BASIC GRAMMAR IN ACTION

An Integrated Course in English

BARBARA H. FOLEY

ELIZABETH R. NEBLETT

HEINLE & HEINLE

THOMSON LEARNING™

United States   Australia   Canada   Mexico   Singapore   Spain   United Kingdom

HEINLE & HEINLE

THOMSON LEARNING

Acknowledgments: We wish to thank the faculty and students at the Institute for Intensive English, Union County College, New Jersey, for their support and encouragement during this project. Many faculty members previewed the units in their classrooms, offering suggestions for changes and additions. Students shared stories and compositions, and smiled and posed for numerous photographs. Special thanks to Cesar Jimenez, who graciously invited us into his home and permitted us to take pictures of his family. Grazie to Elvira DiMauro for her delicious meals and smiling picture. Stuart Scott, UCC's security guard, posed as his friendly, helpful self. Once again, Cao and Nguyet Le were available to try out different professions for our camera. Thanks to our reviewers Tracy J. von Maluski, Dona Ana Branch Community College; Maria Miranda, Lindsey Hopkins Technical Education Center; and George L. Myskiw, Ukrainian–American Club School of English. Thanks, also, to the staff at Heinle & Heinle, who remained encouraging and calm throughout the development and production of this text.

**Vice President,
Editorial Director ESL/EFL:**
Nancy Leonhardt

Acquisitions Editor:
Eric Bredenberg

Developmental Editor:
Thomas Healy

Sr. Production Editor:
Maryellen E. Killeen

Marketing Manager:
Amy Mabley

Manufacturing Manager:
Marcia Locke

Design/Production:
Laurel Technical Services

Cover Design:
Carole Rollins

Cover Image:
Rotunda Design

Printer/Binder:
Courier Stoughton

Illustration:
Dave Blanchette

Library of Congress Cataloging-in-Publication Data
Foley, Barbara H.
Basic grammar in action : an integrated course in English / Barbara H. Foley, Elizabeth R. Neblett.—
p. cm.
ISBN 0-8384-1119-3
1. English language—Textbooks for foreign speakers. 2. English language—Grammar—Problems, exercises, etc. I. Neblett, Elizabeth R. II. Title.
PE1128.F557   2000
428.2'4—dc21   00-057223

This book is printed on acid-free paper.

ASIA:
Thomson Learning
60 Albert Street, #15-01
Albert Complex
Singapore 189969
Tel   65 336-6411
Fax   65 336-7411

AUSTRALIA/NEW ZEALAND:
Nelson/Thomson Learning
102 Dodds Street
South Melbourne
Victoria 3205
Australia
Tel   61 (0)3 9685-4111
Fax   61 (0)3 9685-4199

LATIN AMERICA:
Thomson Learning
Seneca 53
Colonia Polanco
11560 Mexico, D.F. Mexico
Tel   (525) 281-2906
Fax   (525) 281-2656

CANADA:
Nelson/Thomson Learning
1120 Birchmount Road
Toronto, Ontario
Canada M1K 5G4
Tel   (416) 752-9100
Fax   (416) 752-8102

UK/EUROPE/MIDDLE EAST/AFRICA:
Thomson Learning
Berkshire House
168-173 High Holborn
London WC1V 7AA
United Kingdom
Tel   44 (0)171 497-1422
Fax   44 (0)171 497-1426

SPAIN (includes Portugal):
Thomson Learning/Paraninfo
Calle Magallanes 25
28015 Madrid
España
Tel   34 (0)91 446-3350
Fax   34 (0)91 445-6218

Photo Credits: All photos courtesy of Elizabeth R. Neblett with the following exceptions:
p. 34: © STONE/ Pierre Choiniere, © STONE/ Stewart Cohen, © STONE/ Gary W. Nolton, © STONE/ John Riley, © STONE/ Bob Torrez; p. 41: © STONE/ Dale Durfee, © STONE/ Ken Fisher; p.109: © Chuck Savage/TSM; p.174: © STONE/Peter Cade, © STONE/ HOM, © George Shelley/TSM, © Tom Stewart/TSM; p.178: PhotoDisc, Inc.; p. 203: © STONE/ Daniel Bosler, © George Shelley/ TSM.

Table of Contents

Unit 1: Hello   2

Dictionary: One to Ten

Saying hello and good-bye
Identifying the letters of the alphabet
Giving your name and country
Identifying the numbers 1 to 10
Giving your telephone number
The Big Picture: My Classmates
Writing about classmates

Present tense: *Be*
He and *She*
Possessive pronouns: *my, his, her*
Wh-questions: *What's your name? Where are you from?*

Unit 2: The Classroom   18

Dictionary: Classroom objects

Identifying classroom objects
Identifying the numbers 1 to 30
Describing a classroom
The Big Picture: The Classroom
Looking at Forms: School Registration
Writing about your classroom

Present tense: *Be*
Yes/No questions with *Is*
Singular and plural nouns
There is/there are
Prepositions: *in, on*

Unit 3: The Family   32

Dictionary: The family, Months

Expressing family relationships
Asking and giving ages
Describing a family
Giving your date of birth
Recognizing the ordinals 1st to 31st
The Big Picture: Margaret's Family
Looking at Forms: Basic Information
Writing about your family

Present tense: *Be*
How old questions
Present tense questions: *Where does he live? Where do they live?*
Preposition: *in*

Unit 4: At Home   44

Dictionary: At Home

Describing a house
Identifying furniture
Describing home activities
Giving your address
Addressing an envelope
The Big Picture: Where Is Everybody?
Looking at Forms: Change-of-Address Form
Writing about your home

Statements with *need/have*
Where questions: *Where do you want this chair?*
Present continuous statements
Wh-questions: *Where is he? What's he doing?*

Unit 5: Downtown   60

Dictionary: Stores, Places, Locations

Naming places in a town
Describing locations
Talking about the public library
The Big Picture: Downtown
Looking at Forms: Library Card Application
Writing about the library

Prepositions: *across from, behind, on the corner of, between, on, next to*
Where questions: *Where are the children's books?*
Where can I . . . ? questions
Present continuous tense

Unit 6: Working at the Mall   74

Dictionary: Jobs

Naming jobs in a mall
Describing a worker's responsibilities
Telling time
Naming the days of the week
Understanding a work schedule
Describing a busy day
The Big Picture: The CD Den
Looking at Forms: A Work Application
Writing about the CD Den; A Busy Day

Present tense statements
Yes/No questions with *Does*
Where and *What* questions: *Where does she work?*
    What does she do?
What time questions
Prepositions: *at; from-to*

Unit 7: Money   90

Dictionary: Coins, Bills

Stating amounts
Giving the price
Writing a check
Naming stores in your community
Discussing sales
Talking about saving money
The Big Picture: A Yard Sale
Looking at Numbers: Figuring the Change
Writing about saving money

Prices: *It's $1.25.*
How much questions: *How much is it? How much are they?*
Present tense statements

Unit 8: Shopping and Recreation   106

Dictionary: Clothing

Identifying articles of clothing
Asking about price
Shopping in a clothing store
Shopping in a sporting goods store
The Big Picture: At the Park
Looking at Numbers: Figuring the Price
Writing about the park

Present continuous statements
Wh-questions: *What's he wearing?*
How much questions

Unit 9: Food   118

Dictionary: Breakfast, Lunch, Dinner, Beverages, Fruit, Dessert

Talking about food likes and dislikes
Describing meals
Reading a lunch menu
Ordering lunch
Naming restaurants in your community
The Big Picture: At a Restaurant
Looking at Numbers: Figuring Out a Bill

Present tense statements
Present tense negatives
Yes/No questions with *Do*
Wh-questions: *What do you eat for breakfast?*
Always, sometimes, never
Present continuous tense

Unit 10: Finding an Apartment   132

Dictionary: Adjectives, Inside the apartment, Apartment problems

Describing an apartment
Reading a classified ad
Calling the super
Describing an apartment problem
Calling about an apartment for rent
The Big Picture: My Neighborhood
Looking at Forms: The Bottom Part of a Lease
Writing about your home

Adjectives
There is/There are
Means: *Apt. means apartment.*
Must/Must not
Yes/No questions
Present continuous tense

Unit 11: Applying for a Job 148

Dictionary: Hotel occupations

Identifying hotel occupations	Present tense statements
Describing job responsibilities	Yes/No questions with Do
Stating job skills	Can/Can't
Reading a job ad	Past tense of be: I was a cook.
Understanding salary and benefits	Adjectives
Understanding a job interview	
The Big Picture: The Sunrise Hotel	
Looking at Numbers: Figuring Out Salary	
Looking at Forms: Job Application	
Writing about your job	

Unit 12: Transportation 168

Dictionary: Transportation, Weather

Following directions	Question: How do I get to _____?
Looking at a bus schedule	Must/must not
Talking about the weather	Future tense statements
Describing a bus ride	Present continuous tense
Talking about transportation in your community	Adjectives: It's sunny and warm.
The Big Picture: Traffic	
Looking at Forms: A Parking Ticket	
Writing about transportation and your family	

Unit 13: A Visit to the Doctor 186

Dictionary: Parts of the body, Health problems, Remedies

Identifying parts of the body	When statements: When I have a headache, I take aspirin.
Describing health problems	Present tense: have
Discussing remedies	Present tense statements
Reading medicine labels	Must/must not
Making a doctor's appointment	Future tense statements
Looking at Forms: A Patient Information Form	
Looking at Numbers: Reading a Thermometer	
The Big Picture: In the Waiting Room	
Writing a conversation	

Unit 14: Work Rules 200

Dictionary: Jobs, Tools and Equipment

Identifying jobs and work equipment	Who questions: Who works at a factory?
Describing job responsibilities	Have to/Has to/Don't have to/Doesn't have to
Giving excuses	Past continuous statements
Describing work and safety rules	Yes/No questions with Do
The Big Picture: Inspection at the Factory	Recognizing past tense
Looking at Forms: An Accident Report	
Writing about your job	

Unit 15: School 214

Dictionary: Classroom activities, School subjects

Identifying school subjects and activities	Present continuous
Understanding the American school system	Present tense statements
Discussing classroom behavior	Present tense negatives
Identifying the parts of a computer	Yes/No questions with Do
The Big Picture: In the Classroom	Yes/No questions with Did
Helping your child succeed in school	
Looking at Forms: An Absence Note	
Writing about school	

Tapescripts 230

Guide to Basic Grammar in Action

Basic Grammar in Action, An Integrated Course in English provides the foundation for students to move into *The New Grammar in Action, Book 1.* Each unit progresses from vocabulary development to sentence-level grammatical instruction, preparing students to practice real-world tasks.

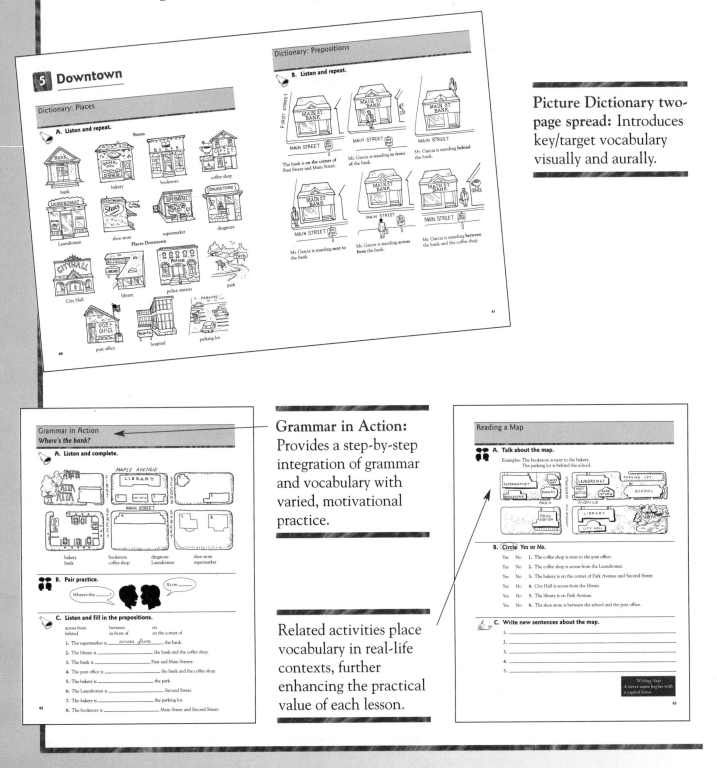

Picture Dictionary two-page spread: Introduces key/target vocabulary visually and aurally.

Grammar in Action: Provides a step-by-step integration of grammar and vocabulary with varied, motivational practice.

Related activities place vocabulary in real-life contexts, further enhancing the practical value of each lesson.

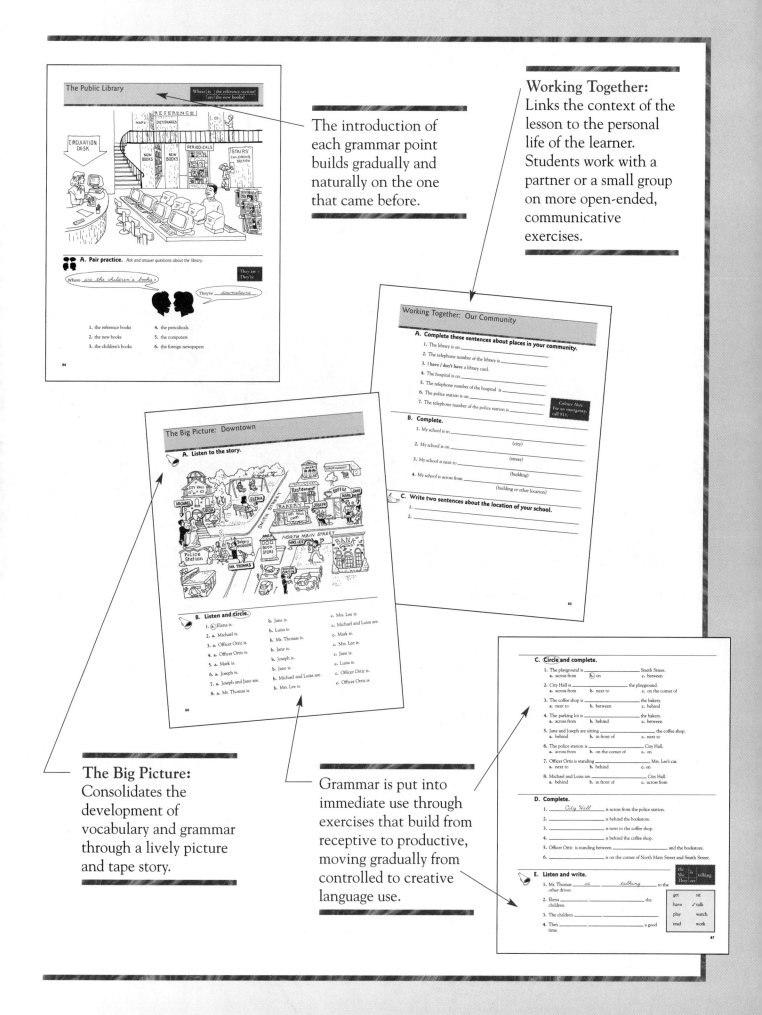

The Public Library

Where is the reference section?
are the new books?

A. **Pair practice.** Ask and answer questions about the library.

Where _are the children's books_?

They're _downstairs_

They are •
They're

1. the reference books
2. the new books
3. the children's books
4. the periodicals
5. the computers
6. the foreign newspapers

64

The introduction of each grammar point builds gradually and naturally on the one that came before.

Working Together:
Links the context of the lesson to the personal life of the learner. Students work with a partner or a small group on more open-ended, communicative exercises.

Working Together: Our Community

A. **Complete these sentences about places in your community.**
1. The library is on _____.
2. The telephone number of the library is _____.
3. I have / don't have a library card.
4. The hospital is on _____.
5. The telephone number of the hospital is _____.
6. The police station is on _____.
7. The telephone number of the police station is _____.

Culture Note
For an emergency, call 911.

B. **Complete.**
1. My school is in _____ (city)
2. My school is on _____ (street)
3. My school is next to _____ (building)
4. My school is across from _____ (building or other location)

C. **Write two sentences about the location of your school.**
1. _____
2. _____

65

The Big Picture: Downtown

A. **Listen to the story.**

B. **Listen and circle.**
1. a. Elena is.   b. Jane is.   c. Mrs. Lee is.
2. a. Michael is.   b. Luisa is.   c. Michael and Luisa are.
3. a. Officer Ortiz is.   b. Mr. Thomas is.   c. Mark is.
4. a. Officer Ortiz is.   b. Jane is.   c. Mrs. Lee is.
5. a. Mark is.   b. Joseph is.   c. Jane is.
6. a. Joseph is.   b. Jane is.   c. Luisa is.
7. a. Joseph and Jane are.   b. Michael and Luisa are.   c. Officer Ortiz is.
8. a. Mr. Thomas is.   b. Mrs. Lee is.   c. Officer Ortiz is.

66

The Big Picture:
Consolidates the development of vocabulary and grammar through a lively picture and tape story.

Grammar is put into immediate use through exercises that build from receptive to productive, moving gradually from controlled to creative language use.

C. **Circle and complete.**
1. The playground is _____ Smith Street.
   a. across from   b. on   c. between
2. City Hall is _____ the playground.
   a. across from   b. next to   c. on the corner of
3. The coffee shop is _____ the bakery.
   a. next to   b. between   c. behind
4. The parking lot is _____ the bakery.
   a. across from   b. behind   c. between
5. Jane and Joseph are sitting _____ the coffee shop.
   a. behind   b. in front of   c. next to
6. The police station is _____ City Hall.
   a. across from   b. on the corner of   c. on
7. Officer Ortiz is standing _____ Mrs. Lee's car.
   a. next to   b. behind   c. on
8. Michael and Luisa are _____ City Hall.
   a. behind   b. in front of   c. across from

D. **Complete.**
1. _City Hall_ is across from the police station.
2. _____ is behind the bookstore.
3. _____ is next to the coffee shop.
4. _____ is behind the coffee shop.
5. Officer Ortiz is standing between _____ and the bookstore.
6. _____ is on the corner of North Main Street and Smith Street.

E. **Listen and write.**
1. Mr. Thomas _is_ _talking_ to the other driver.
2. Elena _____ the children.
3. The children _____.
4. They _____ a good time.

He
She
They

is
are

talking

get   sit
have   ✓talk
play   watch
read   work

67

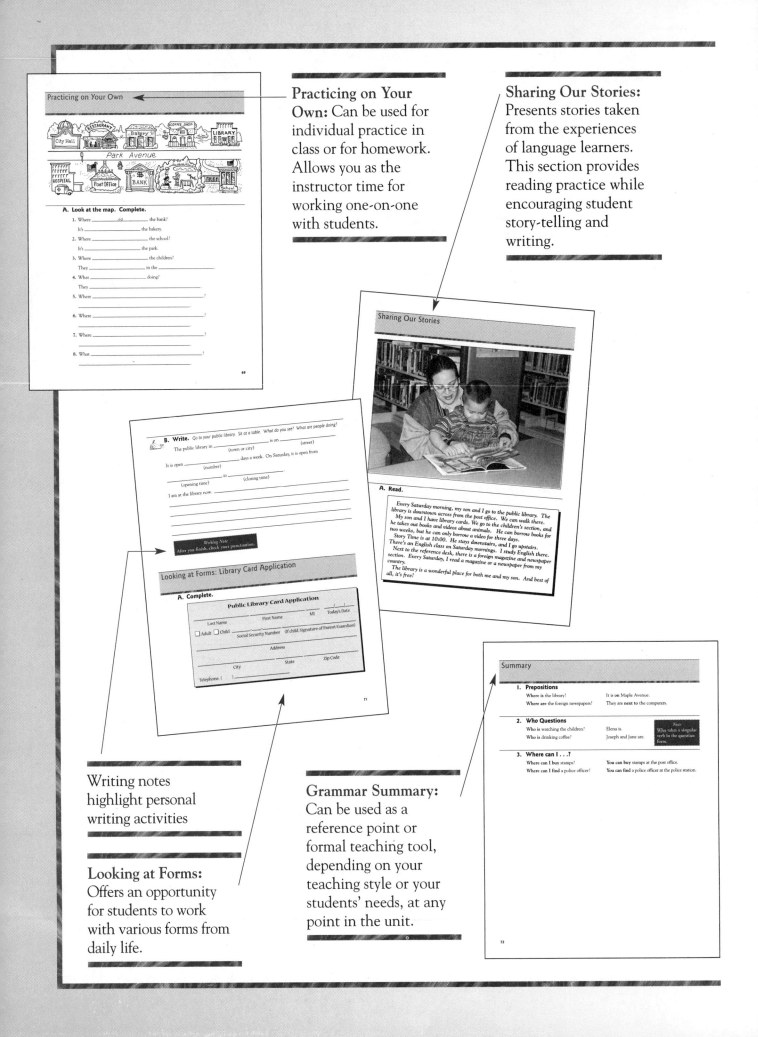

Practicing on Your Own: Can be used for individual practice in class or for homework. Allows you as the instructor time for working one-on-one with students.

Sharing Our Stories: Presents stories taken from the experiences of language learners. This section provides reading practice while encouraging student story-telling and writing.

Writing notes highlight personal writing activities

Looking at Forms: Offers an opportunity for students to work with various forms from daily life.

Grammar Summary: Can be used as a reference point or formal teaching tool, depending on your teaching style or your students' needs, at any point in the unit.

STANDARDS OVERVIEW

BASIC GRAMMAR IN ACTION Units	CASAS Comprehensive Adult Student Assessment System	SCANS Secretary's Commission on Achieving Necessary Skills	EFF Equipped For the Future	NATIONAL STANDARDS L/S = Listening & Speaking R = Reading W = Writing
Unit 1: **Hello**	0.1.4 0.1.6 0.2.1 1.2.2	Basic Skills Interpersonal Skills Manages Information	Communication Skills Interpersonal Skills	L/S: Speak with a few words or sentences W: Complete basic forms with personal information ; W: Capitalize
Unit 2: **The Classroom**	0.1.4 0.1.6	Basic Skills	Interpersonal Skills	L/S: Ask and answer using simple sentences or phrases
Unit 3: **The Family**	0.2.1 1.2.2 1.1.3	Basic Skills Manages Information	Interpersonal, Parent/Family Role	R: Retell simple stories- *Sharing Our Stories* W: Completes forms
Unit 4: **At Home**	0.1.2 1.4.1	Basic Skills Interpersonal Skills	Parent/Family Role	L/S: Ask and answer using simple sentences or phrases
Unit 5: **Downtown**	0.2.2 1.1.3 2.5.6, 2.5.3	Basic Skills, Systems, Manages Information	Interpersonal Skills Citizen Role	R: Understand and follow multi-step oral directions W: Complete basic forms
Unit 6: **Working at the Mall**	1.1.3, 1.2.1 2.3.1, 2.3.2	Basic Skills Manages Resources	Interpersonal, Worker Role	L/S: Speak with a few words or sentences W: Capitalize
Unit 7: **Money**	1.3.1, 1.8.1 1.8.2	Basic Skills Manages Resources	Interpersonal, Citizen Role	R: Uses words and sentences in social context W: Forms
Unit 8: **Shopping and Recreation**	0.2.4, 1.2.3 1.3.9, 1.6.4 2.6.1, 6.4.1	Basic Skills Interpersonal Skills Thinking Skills	Communication, Decision-Making Skills	L/S: Oral instruction through non-verbal responses W: writes narrative in sentences
Unit 9: **Food**	1.3.8, 2.6.4 6.1.1, 6.4.3 6.5.1, 8.2.1	Basic Skills Manages Information	Interpersonal, Communication Skills	L/S: Communicate basic personal need W: Begins to write narratives in sentences
Unit 10: **Finding an Apartment**	1.1.3, 1.4.2 1.4.1, 1.4.3 1.7.5	Basic Skills Interpersonal Skills Thinking Skills	Parent Role Decision-Making Skills	L/S: Follow oral instructions W: Complete business form with personal information
Unit 11: **Applying for a job**	4.1.2 4.1.3 6.1.3 6.5.1	Basic Skills Interpersonal Skills	Worker Role Lifelong Learning Skills	L/S: Ask and answer questions in sentences W: Complete business form with personal information
Unit 12: **Transportation**	1.1.3, 1.9.1 2.2.1, 2.2.2 2.2.3, 2.2.4 2.2.5, 2.3.3 4.8.1	Basic Skills Manages Resources Manages Information	Citizen Role Interpersonal, Communication Skills	R: Understands and follows simple directions W: Begins to write brief narratives in simple sentences
Unit 13: **A Visit to the Doctor**	0.2.2, 3.1.1 3.1.2, 3.1.3 3.2.1, 3.2.3 3.3.1, 3.3.2 3.4.3	Basic Skills Manages Information Personal Qualities	Parent/Family Role Communication Skills	L/S Begins to communicate basic personal needs W: Complete business form with personal information
Unit 14: **Work Rules**	4.1.6, 4.1.8 4.3.1, 4.3.3 4.3.4, 4.4.1 4.4.2, 4.4.4 4.5.1	Basic Skills Interpersonal Skills Systems Management	Worker Role Interpersonal Skills	R: Understands and follows simple directions W: Complete form with personal information
Unit 15: **School**	2.5.5 6.0.1	Basic Skills Personal Qualities Technology	Family Role Communication Skills	R: Ask and answer questions in sentences W: Write brief narratives in sentences

This chart is only a correlation overview. Complete correlations are available from the publisher.

Dictionary

 A. Listen and repeat.

one student

two students

three students

four students

five students

six students

seven students

eight students

nine students

ten students

Grammar in Action

A. Listen.

B. Pair practice.

A: Hello. My name is ____MARIA____.

B: Hi. I'm ____HOSHI____.

A: Nice to meet you.

B: Nice to meet you, too.

> I am = I'm

C. Complete.

My first name is ____MARIA____.

My last name is ____ROJAS____.

Ana Santos
First Name: Ana
Last Name: Santos

The Alphabet

A. Listen.

Aa	Bb	Cc	Dd	Ee	Ff	Gg
Hh	Ii	Jj	Kk	Ll	Mm	Nn
Oo	Pp	Qq	Rr	Ss	Tt	Uu
Vv	Ww	Xx	Yy	Zz		

B. Listen again and repeat.

C. Write.

A	=	capital letter
a	=	lowercase letter

Aa   Bb   Cc   Dd

Ee   Ff   Gg   Hh

Ii   Jj   Kk   Ll

Mm   Nn   Oo   Pp

Qq   Rr   Ss   Tt

Uu   Vv   Ww   Xx

Yy   Zz

4

Please spell that.

A. Listen.

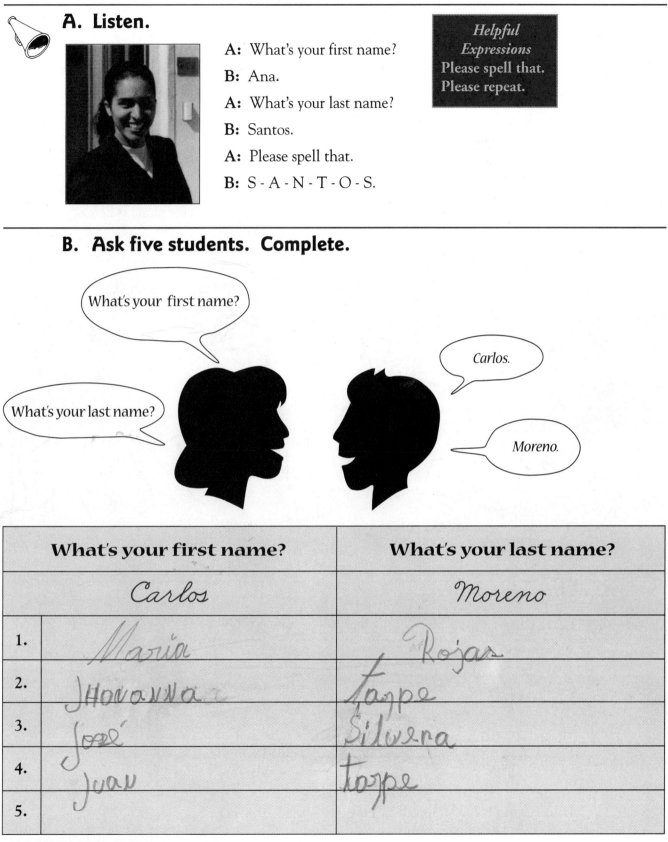

A: What's your first name?

B: Ana.

A: What's your last name?

B: Santos.

A: Please spell that.

B: S - A - N - T - O - S.

B. Ask five students. Complete.

What's your first name?

What's your last name?

Carlos.

Moreno.

	What's your first name?	What's your last name?
	Carlos	*Moreno*
1.	María	Rojas
2.	JHovanna	tarpe
3.	José	Silvera
4.	Juan	tarpe
5.		

5

My Classmates

A. Read.

My name is Ana.

His name is Tuan.

Her name is Erika.

B. Say your classmates' names.

His name is Boris.

Her name is Joanna.

C. Circle *His* or *Her.*

1. His **(Her)** name is Olga.

2. **(His)** Her name is Diego.

3. His **(Her)** name is Sandra.

4. His **(Her)** name is Ming.

5. **(His)** Her name is Peter.

Where are you from?

A. Complete.

What's your name?   My name is _____Maria_____.

Where are you from?   I'm from _____PERU_____.

B. Listen.

What's her name?

Her name is Ana.

Where is she from?

She is from Mexico.

What's his name?

His name is Luis.

Where is he from?

He is from Colombia.

C. Match.

1. What's his name?   • Her name is Roya.

2. Where is he from?   • His name is Carlos.

3. What's her name?   • She is from India.

4. Where is she from?   • He is from Colombia.

D. Pair practice. *Ask about each person's name and country.*

1. Ecuador

Monica

2. Kenya

Moses

3. Japan

Yumi

4. Poland

Ela

5. Vietnam

Tuan

6. Cuba

Martin

7

Numbers 1–10

A. Listen.

0	1	2	3	4	5	6	7	8	9	10
zero oh	one	two	three	four	five	six	seven	eight	nine	ten

B. Listen and repeat.

C. Write.

a. ten _____10_____

b. six _____6_____

c. eight _____8_____

d. one _____1_____

e. three _____3_____

f. zero _____0_____

g. two _____2_____

h. four _____4_____

i. seven _____7_____

j. nine _____9_____

k. five _____5_____

D. Listen and circle.

a. 0   (1)   3

b. 3   4   (8)

c. 2   3   10

d. 0   (1)   10

e. (3)   5   7

f. 4   5   6

g. 1   7   9

h. 4   5   9

i. (2)   3   10

j. 6   (8)   10

What's your telephone number?

A. Listen.

A: What's your name?

B: Ana Santos.

A: And your telephone number?

B: 301-824-1796.

A: 301-824-1796?

B: Yes.

A: Thank you.

> *Culture Note*
> In a telephone number, say each number separately.

B. Listen and write.

a. 8 8 3 - 3 2 3 1

b. 636-3290

c. 914-6991

d. 830-2010

e. 212-822-0555

f. 394-866-9210

g. 098-765-4321

h. 718-850-9224
2384579454

C. Pair practice. *Say these telephone numbers with a partner.*

a. 549-8320

b. 668-2390

c. 271-5636

d. 965-8124

e. 908-483-9932

f. 201-977-3425

g. 617-322-9898

h. 212-554-7335

A. Listen.

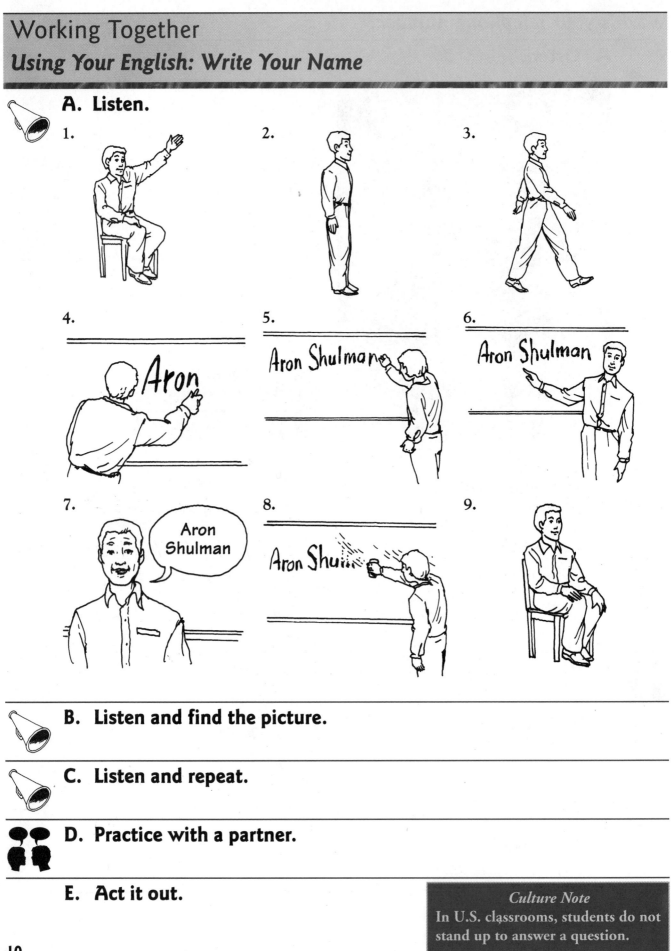

1.
2.
3.
4.
5.
6.
7.

Aron
Shulman

8.
9.

B. Listen and find the picture.

C. Listen and repeat.

D. Practice with a partner.

E. Act it out.

Culture Note
In U.S. classrooms, students do not stand up to answer a question.

10

A. Ask five students these questions. Complete.

What's your name?

Where are you from?

Carlos.

I am from Colombia.

Name	Country
Carlos	Colombia
1. Betty	Perú
2. Eva	Guatemala
3. Maria	Perú
4. José	Chile
5. Martin	México

B. Write about the students.

1. _Carlos_ is from _Colombia_.
2. _Betty_ is from _Perú_.
3. _Eva_ is from _Guatemala_
4. _Maria_ is from _Perú_.
5. _José_ is from _Chile_.
6. I am from _Perú_.

The Big Picture: My Classmates

A. Listen.

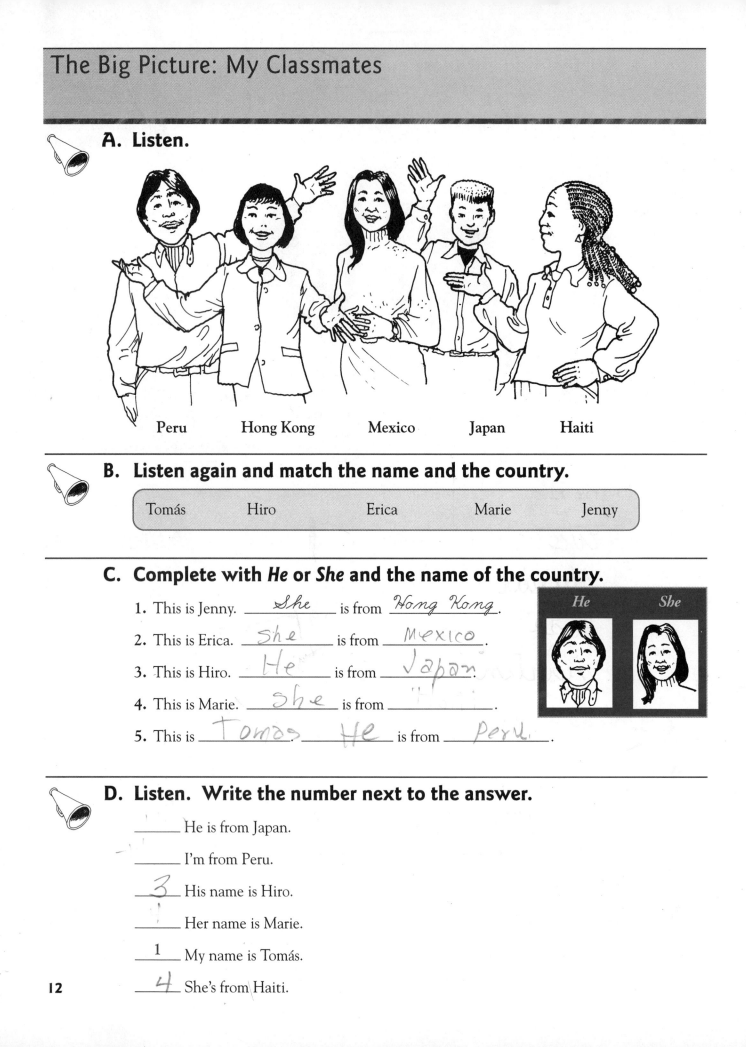

Peru   Hong Kong   Mexico   Japan   Haiti

B. Listen again and match the name and the country.

Tomás   Hiro   Erica   Marie   Jenny

C. Complete with *He* or *She* and the name of the country.

1. This is Jenny. _____She_____ is from _Hong Kong_.
2. This is Erica. _____She_____ is from _____Mexico_____.
3. This is Hiro. _____He_____ is from _____Japan_____.
4. This is Marie. _____She_____ is from _____.
5. This is _____Tomas_____. _____He_____ is from _____Peru_____.

He   *She*

D. Listen. Write the number next to the answer.

_____ He is from Japan.

_____ I'm from Peru.

___3___ His name is Hiro.

___1___ Her name is Marie.

___1___ My name is Tomás.

___4___ She's from Haiti.

12

A. Complete.

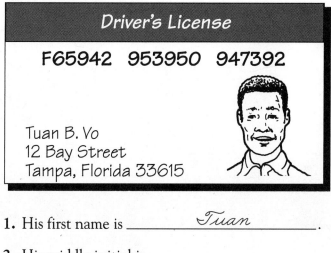

Driver's License

F65942 953950 947392

Tuan B. Vo
12 Bay Street
Tampa, Florida 33615

1. His first name is _____ *Tuan* _____.

2. His middle initial is _____.

3. His last name is _____.

Ana M. Santos
first name: Ana
middle initial: M.
last name: Santos

Edison High School

Student ID

Luisa P. Reyes

ID: 443887

1. Her first name is _____.

2. Her middle initial is _____.

3. Her last name is _____.

4. Her student ID number is _____.

5. Luisa is a student at _____.

B. Match.

1. What's his name?   Her name is Imelda.

2. Where is he from?   He is from Mexico.

3. What's her name?   His name is Hector.

4. Where is she from?   I'm from Poland.

5. What's your name?   She is from the Philippines.

6. Where are you from?   My name is Dorota.

Sharing Our Stories

A. Read.

Hello. My name is Rosa. I'm a student at Eastside Adult School. I study English at night. Luis and Jenny are two students in my class. Luis is from Colombia. Jenny is from Hong Kong. I am from Cuba. We study together.

Rosa

Writing Note
A name begins with a capital letter.
Rosa   Luis

 B. Write about two or three students in your class.

C. Complete.

Writing Note
Always print on forms.

Name: _María_ _____
           last   first

Telephone: __ __ __ - __ __ __ - __ __ __ __

Name: _____ _____
           first   last

Telephone(_____)-_____-_____

Last name									First name													
Telephone			–			–																	

Name: _is María_ ___ _____
         first   initial   last

Telephone:(_914_)-_____-_712-3790_

15

Good-Bye

A. Listen.

B. Pair practice.

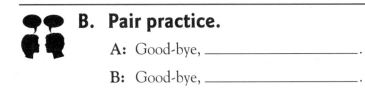

A: Good-bye, _____.

B: Good-bye, _____.

A: See you tomorrow.

B: Have a nice day.

Summary

1. Statements: _be_

I **am** a student.

He **is** a student.

She **is** a student.

Contractions

I am = I'm

He is = He's

She is = She's

2. Possessive pronouns

My name is Ana.

His name is Dan.

Her name is Maria.

3. _Wh-_ questions

What's your name?

Where are you from?

My name is Carlos.

I'm from Colombia.

2 The Classroom

A. Listen and repeat.

clock
wall
map
window
computer
chalkboard
door
piece of chalk
eraser
student
table
teacher
desk
chair
pencil sharpener

18

B. Listen and repeat.

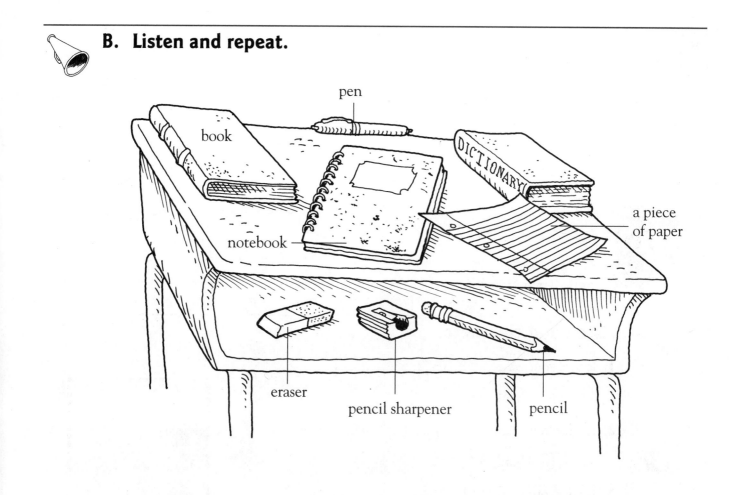

pen

book

DICTIONARY

a piece
of paper

notebook

eraser

pencil sharpener

pencil

C. Check (✓) the items in _your_ classroom.

_____ a table

_____ a chair

_____ desks

_____ a map of the United States

_____ a map of the world

_____ a clock

_____ a computer

_____ a pencil sharpener

_____ a chalkboard

_____ a piece of chalk

_____ an eraser

_____ _____

_____ _____

_____ _____

Grammar in Action
Is this your book?

A. Listen. Number the conversations.

1.
2.
3.

> Is this your
> book?
> Yes, it is.
> No, it isn't.

1. _yes it is_
2. _1_
3. _no it isnt_

B. Listen and complete.

1. Is this your _dictionary_?

   Yes, it is. Thank you.

2. Is this your _pen_?

   Yes, it is. Thank you.

3. Is this your _paper_?

   No, it isn't.

4. Is this your _notebook_?

   Yes, _it is_. Thank you.

5. Is this your _pencil sharpener_

   No, _____ _____.

> pen
>
> paper
>
> dictionary
>
> notebook
>
> pencil sharpener

C. Pair practice.

Is this
your _pencil_ ?

Yes, it is.
Thank you.

Is this
your _table_ ?

No, it isn't.

1. _pencil_
2. _notebook_
3. _table_
4. _dictionary_

20

A book - Books

A. Listen and repeat.

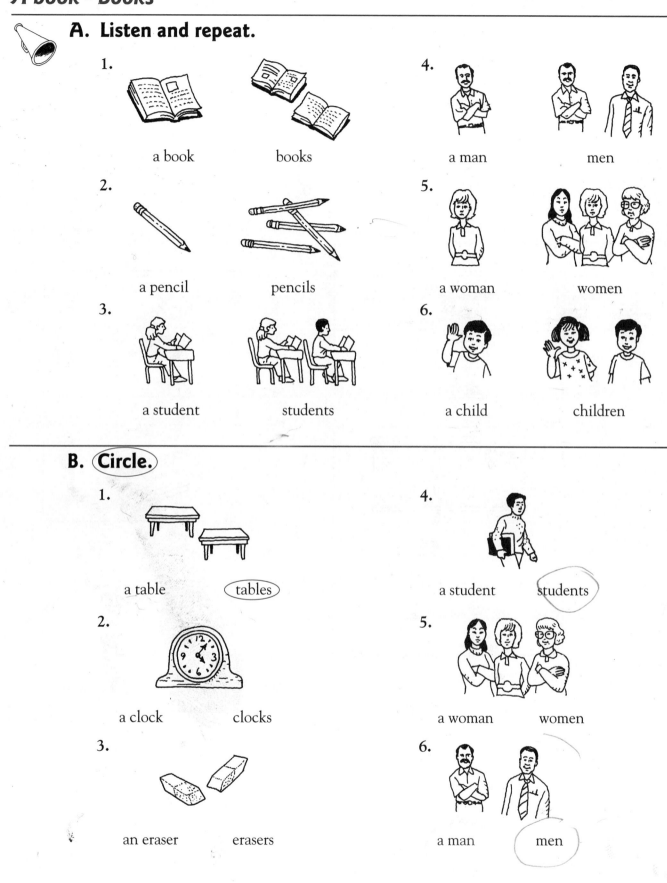

1. a book   books

2. a pencil   pencils

3. a student   students

4. a man   men

5. a woman   women

6. a child   children

B. Circle.

1. a table   (tables)

2. a clock   clocks

3. an eraser   erasers

4. a student   (students)

5. a woman   women

6. a man   (men)

A pencil - Pencils

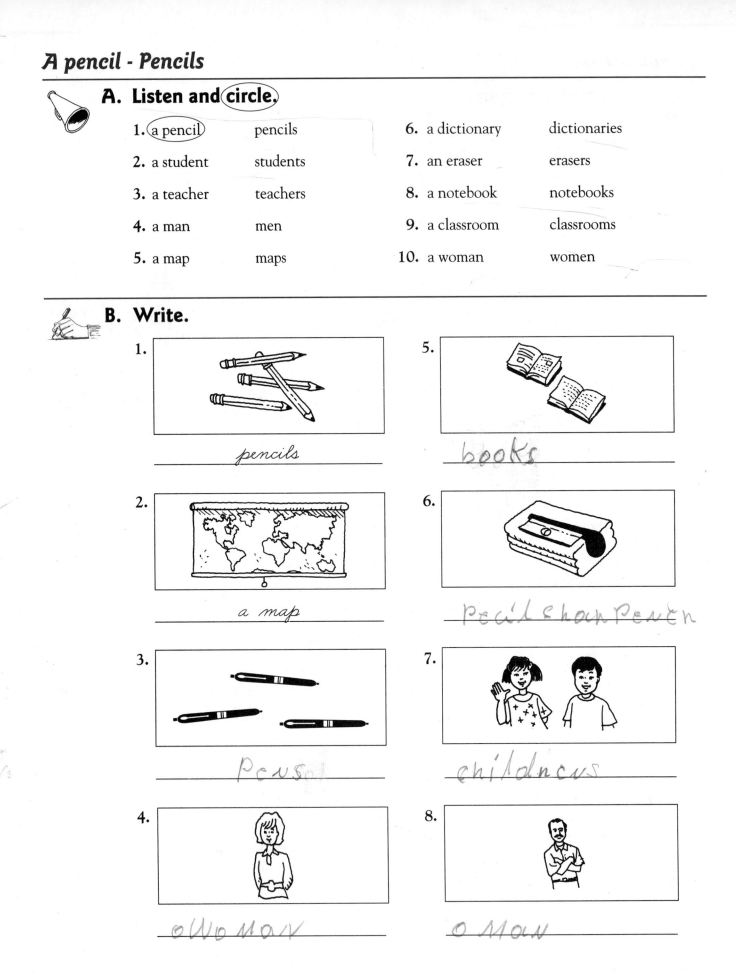

A. Listen and circle.

1. (a pencil)   pencils
2. a student   students
3. a teacher   teachers
4. a man   men
5. a map   maps

6. a dictionary   dictionaries
7. an eraser   erasers
8. a notebook   notebooks
9. a classroom   classrooms
10. a woman   women

B. Write.

1. _pencils_

2. _a map_

3. _Pensol_

4. _a woman_

5. _books_

6. _Pecil shon Penen_

7. _childncus_

8. _a man_

22

Numbers 1–30

A. Listen.

1 one	2 two	3 three	4 four	5 five	6 six	7 seven	8 eight	9 nine	10 ten
11 eleven	12 twelve	13 thirteen	14 fourteen	15 fifteen	16 sixteen	17 seventeen	18 eighteen	19 nineteen	20 twenty
21 twenty-one	22 twenty-two	23 twenty-three	24 twenty-four	25 twenty-five	26 twenty-six	27 twenty-seven	28 twenty-eight	29 twenty-nine	30 thirty

B. Listen and repeat.

C. Listen and point to the number.

D. Listen and circle.

a. 4 (5) 6   e. 12 (17) 18   i. 21 22 (27)

b. 3 4 (9)   f. 14 (16) 18   j. 22 27 (29)

c. (4) 8 9   g. 13 15 (17)   k. 24 25 (26)

d. 2 (3) 10   h. (11) 12 20   l. (21) 25 28

E. Write the number.

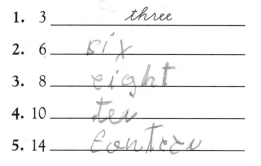

1. 3 _____three_____

2. 6 _____six_____

3. 8 _____eight_____

4. 10 _____ten_____

5. 14 _____fourteen_____

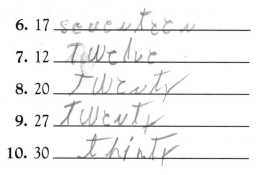

6. 17 _____seventeen_____

7. 12 _____Twelve_____

8. 20 _____Twenty_____

9. 27 _____Twenty_____

10. 30 _____thirty_____

There is - There are

A. Listen.

B. Look at the desk. Listen and circle.

There	is a	book	on the table.
	are	books	

1. Yes (No)   4. Yes (No)
2. Yes (No)   5. Yes (No)
3. (Yes) No   6. Yes (No)

C. Look at the desk above. Complete.

1. There is one _____ notebook _____ on the desk.

2. There are two _____ penciel _____ on the desk.

3. There are five _____ boolrs _____ on the desk.

4. There is one _a picect of papenof_ of paper on the desk.

D. Complete about _your_ class. Use _is_ or _are_ and the number.

1. There _is_ _one_ teacher in our classroom.

2. There _____ _one_ chairs in our classroom.

3. There _are_ _are_ desks in our classroom.

4. There _a mau_ _men_ pencil sharpener in our classroom.

5. There _are_ _fonteou_ students in our class.

6. There _are_ _fiue_ men in our class.

7. There _one_ _viny_ women in our class.

A. Try this. Put 2 or 3 items from each student on a desk.

Student 1: Is this your cell phone?

Student 2: No, it isn't.

Student 1: Is this your cell phone?

Student 3: No, it isn't.

Student 1: Is this your cell phone?

Student 4: Yes, it is.

dbcp

tobe bk

B. Interview two students. (Circle) their answers.

	Partner 1:		Partner 2:	
	_____		_____	
Do you have a dictionary?	Yes, I do.	No, I don't.	Yes, I do.	No, I don't.
Do you have an eraser?	Yes, I do.	No, I don't.	Yes, I do.	No, I don't.
Do you have a piece of paper?	Yes, I do.	No, I don't.	Yes, I do.	No, I don't.
Do you have a pencil sharpener?	Yes, I do.	No, I don't.	Yes, I do.	No, I don't.
Do you have a pen?	Yes, I do.	No, I don't.	Yes, I do.	No, I don't.
Do you have a pencil?	Yes, I do.	No, I don't.	Yes, I do.	No, I don't.

C. Draw a *large* picture of your classroom. Label everything.

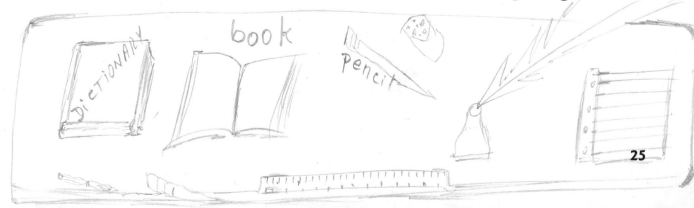

book

Pencil

DICTIONARY

The Big Picture: The Classroom

A. Circle the things you see in this classroom.

a computer   a clock   a map of the United States

a chalkboard   a book   desks

a table   a door   a window

a pencil sharpener   a pencil   a man

a woman   a teacher   a child

B. Listen.

C. Listen and circle.

1. Yes (No)
2. Yes No
3. Yes No
4. Yes No
5. Yes No

6. Yes No
7. Yes No
8. Yes No
9. Yes No
10. Yes No

D. Complete. Write *is* or *are* and the number.

1. There _are_ _ten_ students in this class.

2. There _____ _____ men

and _____ women.

3. There _____ _____ teacher, Mr. Wilson.

4. There _____ _____ desks.

5. There _____ _____ maps on the wall.

6. There _____ _____ clock on the wall.

There	is	one
		two
	are	three
		four

E. Complete.

clock	clocks	student	students
map	✓ maps	man	men
woman	women	desk	desks

1. There are two _maps_ on the wall.

2. There is a _Map_ of the world.

3. There are ten _students_ in the class.

4. There are four _Women men_ and six _Woman_ .

5. There is one _student_ from Korea.

6. There are twelve _clock desks_ in the room.

7. There is a _clock_ on the wall.

Practicing on Your Own

A. Write.

1. 10 _____ten_____
2. 14 _fourteen_
3. 18 _eighteen_
4. 19 _nineteen_
5. 20 _twenty_

6. 22 _twenty-two_
7. 25 _twenty-five_
8. 27 _twenty-seven_
9. 29 _twenty-nine_
10. 30 _thirty_

B. Complete.

> **Is this your book?**
> **Yes, it is.**
> **No, it isn't.**

1. Is this your pencil?   Yes, it ___is___.
2. Is this your dictionary?   No, ___it isn't___.
3. Is this your computer?   Yes, ___it is___.
4. Is this your classroom?   Yes, ___it is___.
5. ___Is___ this your notebook? ___yes, it is___.
6. ___Is___ ___this___ your ___book___? ___yes___, ___it___ ___is___.
7. ___Is___ ___this___ your ___pencil___? ___yes___, ___it___ ___is___.

C. Complete. Write *There is* or *There are*.

> *Writing Note*
> **Begin a sentence**
> **with a capital letter.**

1. ___There___ ___are___ twenty students in our class.
2. ___There___ ___are___ twelve students from my country.
3. ___There___ ___is___ one student from China.
4. ___there___ ___is___ a map of the world on the wall.
5. ___There___ ___are___ two doors in our classroom.
6. ___there___ ___is___ a large table in the classroom.
7. ___There___ ___is___ a computer on the table.
8. ___there___ ___is___ a chalkboard on the wall.
9. ___there___ ___are___ two erasers on the chalkboard.

Sharing Our Stories

A. Read.

> **Writing Note**
> Use a period at the end of a sentence.

    I study English at the English Adult School. My class is large. It's very large. There are 30 students in my class. We are from 20 different countries. We speak 10 different languages.

    Our classroom is small. There are 30 small desks. Our teacher, Mrs. Garcia, has a large desk for her books and her papers. We have many pencils, but we don't have a pencil sharpener. We are from many countries, but we don't have a map on the wall.

    We need a larger classroom with a pencil sharpener and a map.

B. Write. Complete this story about your classroom. *Your teacher will help you write the story together.*

I study English at ___San grouivel___. There are ___twenty two___ students in my class. We are from ___six___ different countries. We speak ___one three___ different languages.

Our classroom is _____. There are _____ ___co chairs___ ___xc twenty dnr___ _____

_____.

A. Complete.

SCHOOL REGISTRATION

Last name: _Rojos_   First name: _Maria_

STUDENT IS REGISTERED FOR:

Class: _____   Room: _47 p.4_

Teacher: _ingles_   Date: _11/18/01_

My School

B. Walk around the school with your teacher. *Check the places you see.*

_____ library

_____ cafeteria

_____ bookstore

_____ stairs

_____ men's room

_____ women's room *or* ladies' room

_____ computer lab

_____ student lounge

_____ _____

Summary

1. *Yes/No* questions

Is this your book?　　　　Yes, it **is.**　　No, it **isn't.**

2. Singular and plural nouns

Regular	*Irregular*
book - book**s**	man - m**e**n
map - map**s**	woman - wom**e**n
student - student**s**	child - child**ren**

3. *There is/There are*

There is a book on the table.

There are three books on the table.

3 Family

Dictionary

A. Listen and repeat.

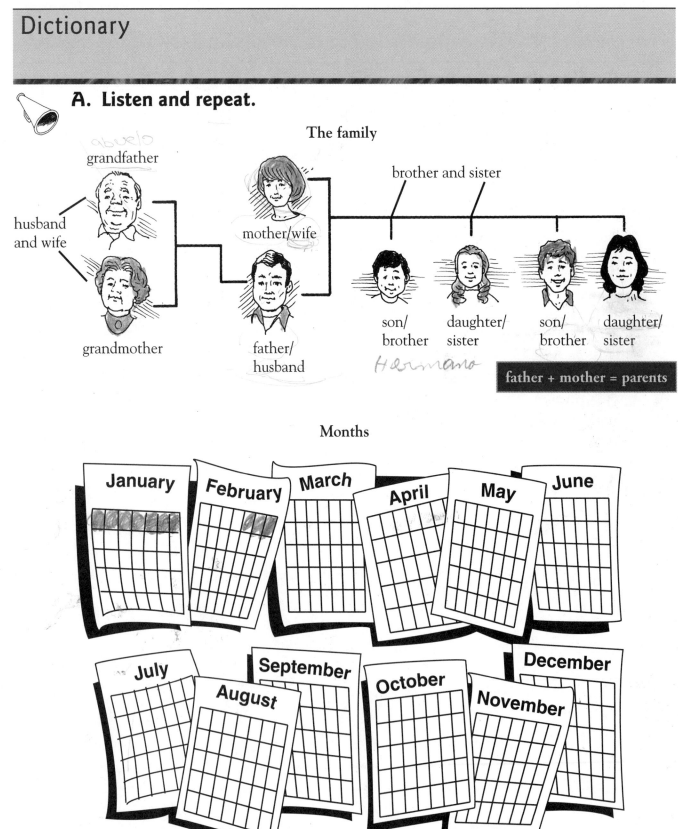

The family

grandfather *(abuelo)*

husband and wife

mother/wife

brother and sister

grandmother

father/husband

son/brother *(Hermano)*

daughter/sister

son/brother

daughter/sister

father + mother = parents

Months

January February March April May June

July August September October November December

Grammar in Action

This is my family.

B. Listen again and complete.

daughter	sons	brothers	daughter
parents	wife	✓ family	children

Hi. That's me in the first picture. My name is Carlos. This is my _____family_____.

This is my _____wife_____. Her name is Maria. These are my _____children_____. I have

two _____sons_____ and one _____daughter_____. Robert is 14, George is 11, and Katie

is 6. These are my _____parents_____, Roberto and Silvia. And these are my two

_____, Tomás and Eric. Tomás is 20, and Eric is 24.

How old is he?

A. Listen and read.

Margaret: This is my son Paul.

Kathy: How old is he?

Margaret: He's 7. And this is my daughter, Gloria.

Kathy: How old is she?

Margaret: She's 16.

Kathy: You have a beautiful family.

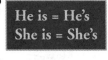

How old is he?
He is 10.

B. Look at the photos in Part C. How old is each person?

He is = He's
She is = She's

How old is she?

I think she's 5.

C. Listen to the conversations. Number the photos.

_____

_____

_____

_____

Culture Note
We ask the ages of children and young people. We do not ask the age of an adult.

34

My Family

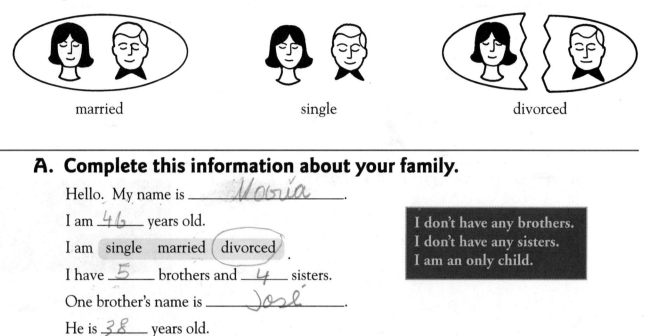

married single divorced

A. Complete this information about your family.

Hello. My name is ___Maria___.

I am __46__ years old.

I am single married (divorced).

I have __5__ brothers and __4__ sisters.

One brother's name is ___José___.

He is __38__ years old.

He is (single) married divorced.

One sister's name is ___Lidia___.

She is __50__ years old.

She is single married (divorced).

> I don't have any brothers.
> I don't have any sisters.
> I am an only child.

B. Complete this chart about three people in your family.

	Relationship	Name	Age	Marital Status		
	brother	Tony	26	married	(single)	divorced
1.	father	Pelayo	60	(married)	single	divorced
2.	daughter	Jaquelin	27	married	(single)	divorced
3.	son	Juan	16	married	(single)	divorced

C. Tell a partner about three people in your family.

I have a brother.

His name is Tony.

He's 26 years old.

He's single.

Where does he live?

A. Listen and read.

Phoung: I have two brothers and one sister. One brother lives in Vietnam, and one brother lives in New York.

Linda: Where does your sister live?

Phoung: She lives in Texas.

B. Look at the map and answer.

1. Where does Maria live?

2. Where do Mr. and Mrs. Jones live?

3. Where does Peter live? *Texas*

He lives in _____.

She lives in _____.

They live in _____.

4. Where does Lana live?

5. Where do Eva and Stan live?

6. Where do you live?

C. Talk about your family.

I live in _____ .

My parents live in _____ .

My brother lives in _____ .

My sister lives in _____ .

My _____ lives in _____ .

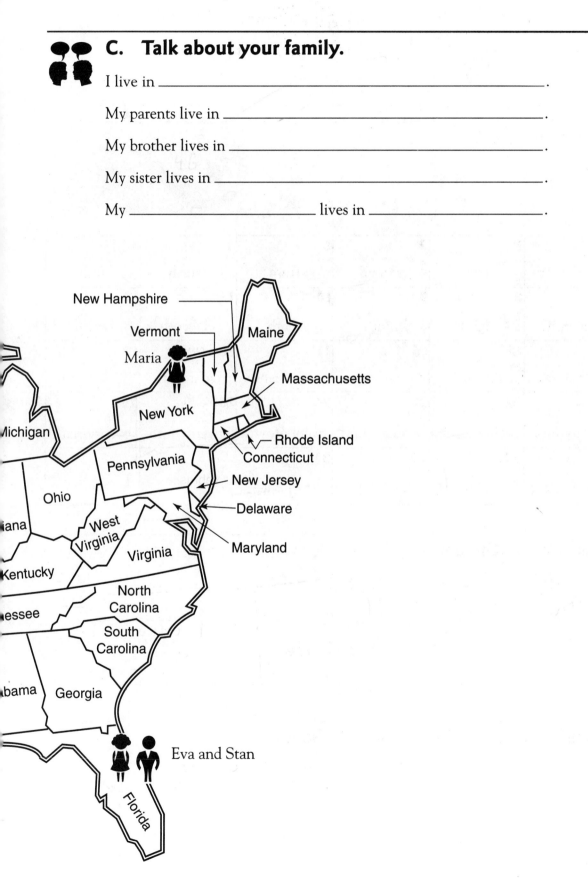

What's your date of birth?

A. Listen.

Date of birth: __9__ / __14__ / __75__
          Month Day Year

Birth Date: | 0 | 3 | 0 | 3 | 8 | 0 |
           Month Date Year

A: What's your date of birth?

B: September 14, 1975.

A: What's your birth date?

B: March 3, 1980.

B. Listen and repeat.

> **Writing Note**
> Months begin with capital letters.
> <u>J</u>anuary   <u>F</u>ebruary

		1 first	**2** second	**3** third	**4** fourth	**5** fifth
6 sixth	**7** seventh	**8** eighth	**9** ninth	**10** tenth	**11** eleventh	**12** twelfth
13 thirteenth	**14** fourteenth	**15** fifteenth	**16** sixteenth	**17** seventeenth	**18** eighteenth	**19** nineteenth
20 twentieth	**21** twenty-first	**22** twenty-second	**23** twenty-third	**24** twenty-fourth	**25** twenty-fifth	**26** twenty-sixth
27 twenty-seventh	**28** twenty-eighth	**29** twenty-ninth	**30** thirtieth	**31** thirty-first		

C. Listen. Write the date.

1. _January 4, 1997_
2. _November 6, 1998_
3. _March 1, 1903_
4. _January 8 2001_

5. _April 11, 2000_
6. _May 29, 1999_
7. _July 30, 1986_
8. _Agust 18, 1903_

D. Sit with a partner. Say the dates above.

What's your date of birth?

Date of birth: ____ / ____ / ____
Month   Day   Year

Working Together: My Family Tree

A. Draw your family tree.

Complete this family tree. Show your parents, your spouse, your children, and your brothers and your sisters. Add more circles if you need to. Write each person's name.

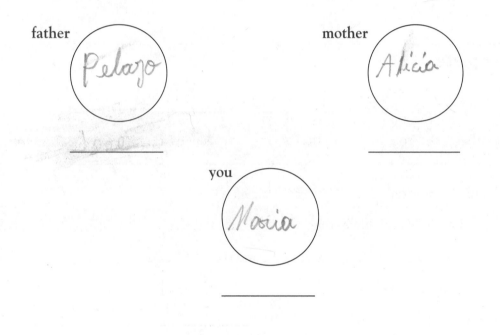

father

Pelayo

_____

mother

Alicia

_____

you

Maria

_____

B. Explain your family tree to a partner.

Examples

This is my mother. Her name is Manisha. She lives in India.

This is my son. His name is Raj. He's 6 years old.

The Big Picture: Margaret's Family

 **A. Listen to Margaret talk about her family.
Write the ages of her children.**

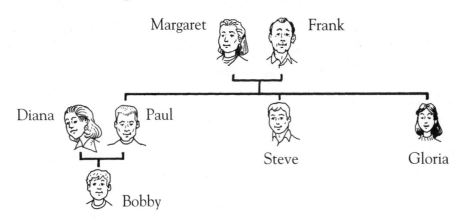

B. Complete.

children	brothers	grandmother	parents
grandfather	son	✓ husband	daughter	sons

1. Frank is Margaret's ___*husband*___.

2. Margaret and Frank have three _____.

3. They have two _____ and one _____.

4. Paul is married. He has a _____, Bobby.

5. Frank and Margaret are Bobby's _____ and _____.

6. Gloria has two _____, Paul and Steve.

7. Her _____ are Frank and Margaret.

C. Listen and circle.

1. (Yes) No	6. Yes No
2. Yes No	7. Yes No
3. Yes No	8. Yes No
4. Yes No	9. Yes No
5. Yes No	10. Yes No

A. Write the answer.

No, she isn't.	She's 23.
He lives in New Jersey.	She lives in Florida.
✓ That's my brother.	His name is Cesar.
Her name is Erica.	He's 26.
Yes, he's married.	That's my sister.

1. Who's this? _____ *That's my brother.* _____

2. What's his name? _____

3. How old is he? _____

4. Where does he live? _____

5. Is he married? _____

6. Who's this? _____

7. What's her name? _____

8. How old is she? _____

9. Where does she live? _____

10. Is she married? _____

B. Write the date.

1. 1/3/95   *January 3, 1995*

2. 4/7/99   *April 7/99*

3. 3/21/86   *March 2 68*

4. 4/8/75   *April 8/1 75*

5. 9/6/68   *Sept*

6. 11/12/00   _____

7. 12/25/05   _____

> *Writing Note*
> Put a comma between the day and the year.
> **January 1, 1995**

A. Read.

This is a photograph of my granddaughter and me. My granddaughter is seven years old. Her name is Jessica. In this picture, it is summer. It is August or early September. We are sitting in the backyard of our house. That's our dog. His name is Sasha. Sasha is only a puppy. He's six months old.

B. Write about a photograph.
Bring in a photograph of your family. Tell a partner about the picture. Write about your photograph.

Looking at Numbers

Name:	*Marta*	*Londono*	*B.*
	first	last	middle intial

Sex: Male (Female) Date of Birth: _11_ _6_ _81_
                                   month date year

How old is Marta? She is _____ years old.

Last name	O R L O V					**First name**	B O R I S							
Birthdate	0 9 – 0 4 – 7 6													

How old is Boris? He is _____ years old.

42

A. Complete.

Name: _____ _____ _____
           first   last   middle intial

Status: single   married   divorced   Sex: male   female

Telephone (_____)-_____-_____

Date of Birth: _____ _____ _____
                month   day   year

Male   Female

NAME (Last, First, Middle)	
MARITAL STATUS Single Married Divorced	SEX Male Female
TELEPHONE NUMBER (include area code) ( ) -	BIRTH DATE ____/____/____ Month Day Year

Last name											First name										
Birthdate		-		-			Telephone	7	1	2	-	3	7	-	9	9		

Summary

1. *How old* questions.

How old **is** he?   He's fifteen.

How old **is** she?   She's seven.

2. Present tense

Where **do** you **live**?   I **live** in California.

Where **do** they **live**?   They **live** in California.

Where **does** he **live**?   He **lives** in California.

Where **does** she **live**?   She **lives** in California.

 **At Home**

Dictionary

A. Listen and repeat.

Rooms

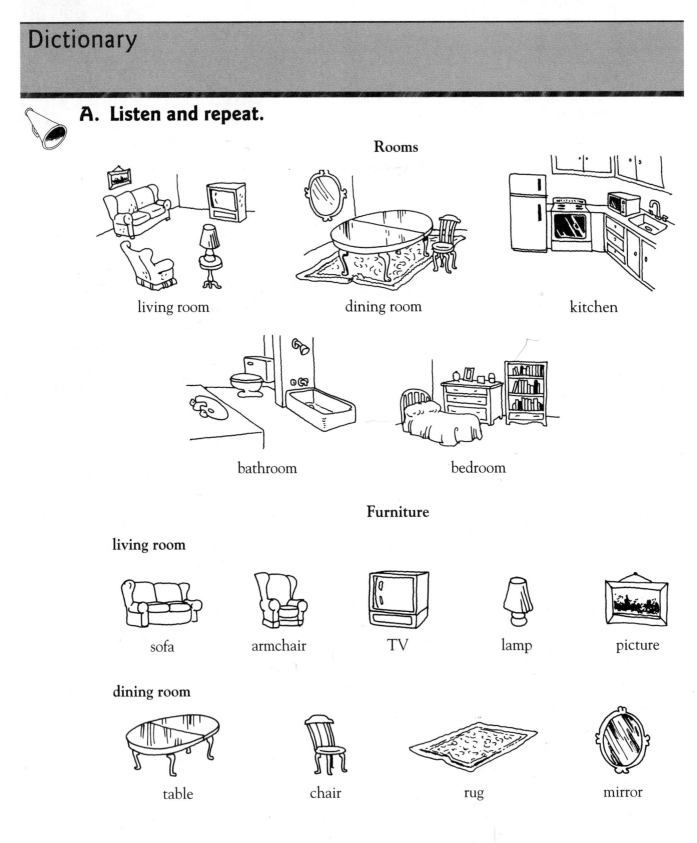

living room

dining room

kitchen

bathroom

bedroom

Furniture

living room

sofa   armchair   TV   lamp   picture

dining room

table   chair   rug   mirror

44

kitchen

stove   sink   microwave   refrigerator

bedroom

bed   dresser   bookcase

bathroom

sink   toilet   bathtub   shower

B. Listen and repeat.

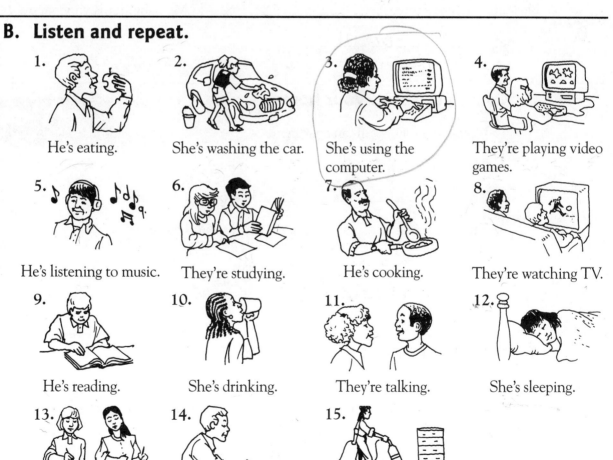

1. He's eating.

2. She's washing the car.

3. She's using the computer.

4. They're playing video games.

5. He's listening to music.

6. They're studying.

7. He's cooking.

8. They're watching TV.

9. He's reading.

10. She's drinking.

11. They're talking.

12. She's sleeping.

13. They're doing their homework.

14. He's writing a letter.

15. She's cleaning the house.

A. Listen and complete.

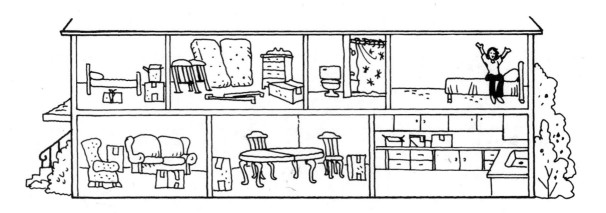

This is our new house. We're moving in today. There is a nice _____*kitchen*_____
and a small __*living room*__. There is a large *dining room* .
Upstairs, there are three _____*bedrooms*_____. My daughter is very happy. Now she
has her own _____*bedroom*_____.

B. Complete about your home.

> There **is one** bedroom.
> There **are two** bedrooms.

1. I live   in a house / (in an apartment.)
2. There are __*five*_____ rooms in my home.
3. There __*are*_____ __*two*_____ bedroom / bedrooms.
4. There _____*is*_____ __*one*_____ bathroom / bathrooms.
5. There is a large __*living room*_____
6. There is a small __*kitchen*_____.

C. Read your sentences to a partner.

D. Talk about these homes. Use your imagination!

46

Moving

A. Listen.

A: Where do you want this armchair?

B: Put the armchair in the living room.

A: Where do you want this lamp?

B: Put the lamp in Jenny's bedroom.

B. Pair practice.

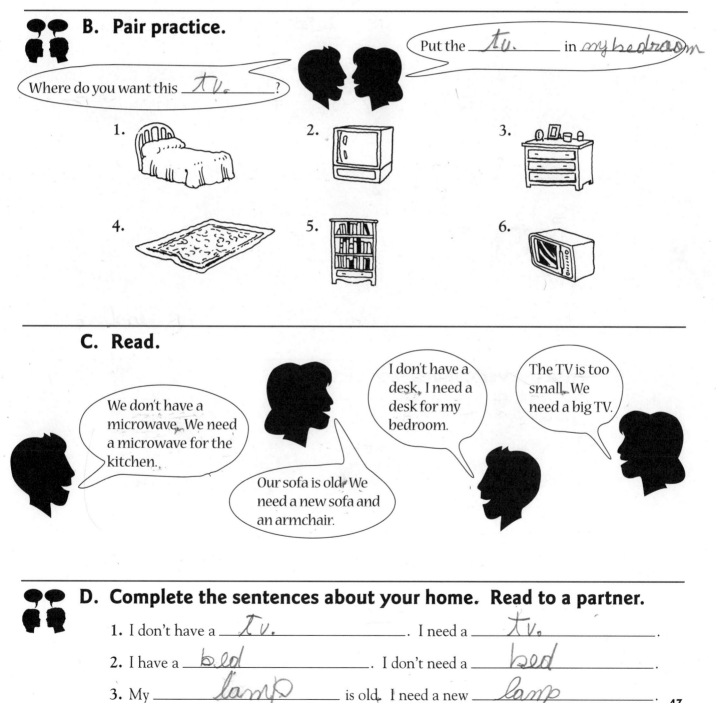

Where do you want this ___t.v.___?

Put the ___t.v.___ in ___my bedroom___

1.

2.

3.

4.

5.

6.

C. Read.

We don't have a microwave. We need a microwave for the kitchen.

Our sofa is old. We need a new sofa and an armchair.

I don't have a desk. I need a desk for my bedroom.

The TV is too small. We need a big TV.

D. Complete the sentences about your home. Read to a partner.

1. I don't have a ___t.v.___. I need a ___t.v.___.

2. I have a ___bed___. I don't need a ___bed___.

3. My ___lamp___ is old. I need a new ___lamp___.

He's reading the newspaper.

A. Listen and repeat.

Present Continuous		
I	am	
He	is	reading.
She		
They	are	

1. _is eating_

2. _is Washing_

3. _is cooking_

4. _are playing_

5. _is using_

6. _are studying_

7. _is sleeping_

8. _are Watching_

9. _is reading_

B. Write the verb under each picture.

is sleeping	is washing	are playing
are studying	✓ is eating	is cooking
is using	is reading	are watching

C. Listen. Write the number of the correct picture.

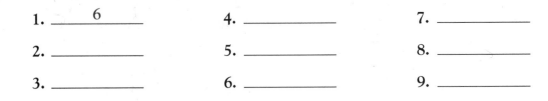

1. ___6___   4. _____   7. _____

2. _____   5. _____   8. _____

3. _____   6. _____   9. _____

Where is he? What's he doing?

A. Match.

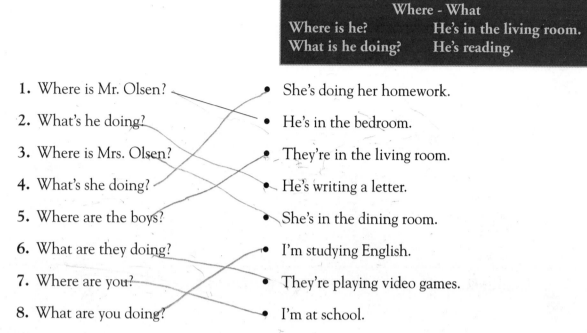

Where - What	
Where is he?	He's in the living room.
What is he doing?	He's reading.

1. Where is Mr. Olsen?
2. What's he doing?
3. Where is Mrs. Olsen?
4. What's she doing?
5. Where are the boys?
6. What are they doing?
7. Where are you?
8. What are you doing?

- She's doing her homework.
- He's in the bedroom.
- They're in the living room.
- He's writing a letter.
- She's in the dining room.
- I'm studying English.
- They're playing video games.
- I'm at school.

B. Pair practice.

Example

A: Where is he?

B: He's in the living room.

A: What's he doing?

B: He is listening to music.

1.

2.

3.

4.

5.

6.

What's your address?

A. Listen and read.

A: What's your address?

B: 419 South Avenue.

A: What town?

B: Cranford.

A: And what's your zip code?

B: 07016.

B. Listen. Repeat the street addresses.

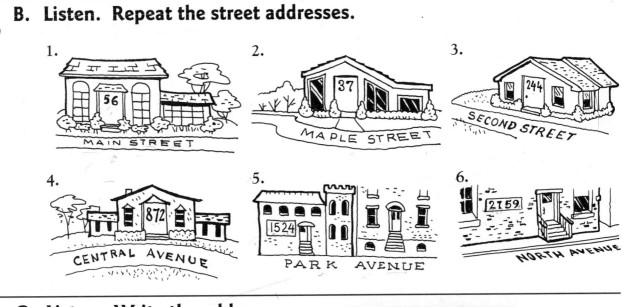

1. 56 MAIN STREET
2. 37 MAPLE STREET
3. 244 SECOND STREET
4. 872 CENTRAL AVENUE
5. 1524 PARK AVENUE
6. 2159 NORTH AVENUE

C. Listen. Write the address.

1. __73__ North Avenue
2. __37__ Maple Street
3. __872__ Central Avenue
4. __1524__ Park Avenue
5. __244__ First Street
6. __56__ Main Street

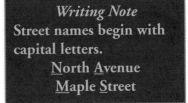

Writing Note
Street names begin with capital letters.
North Avenue
Maple Street

D. Repeat the addresses above with a partner.

Sending a Letter

A. Interview three students.

What's your name?	What's your address?	What's your zip code?
Pierre	349 Pine Place Santa Rosa	03402
1. Rosa	145 Union St.	10801
2. Juan	47 La Wton St. New Rochelle	10801
3. Betty	618 Main Street New Rochelle	10801

B. Read.

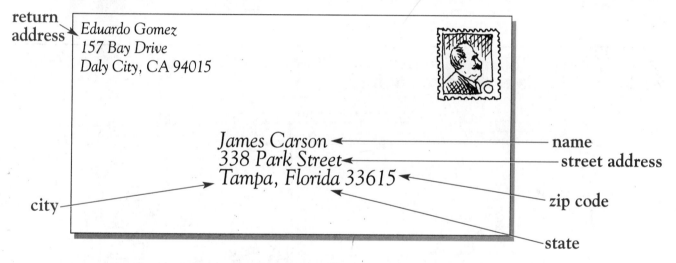

return address → Eduardo Gomez
157 Bay Drive
Daly City, CA 94015

James Carson ← name
338 Park Street ← street address
Tampa, Florida 33615 ← zip code

city → Tampa

state

C. Address this envelope to a friend.

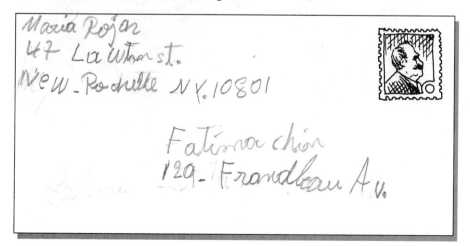

Maria Rojan
47 La Wton st.
New Rochelle NY. 10801

Fatima chon
129 Frandleau Av.

51

A. Check your classmates' activities. Add three sentences.

_____ Someone is writing.

_____ Someone is reading.

_____ Someone is talking.

_____ Someone is drinking a cup of coffee.

_____ Someone is sharpening a pencil.

1. _____

2. _____

3. _____

B. Write. Name each person. Where is each person? What is each person doing?

1. _____

2. _____

3. _____

4. _____

5. _____

6. _____

7. _____

C. The Newspaper

Bring in newspapers from the week. Cut out pictures. What is happening in each picture? Make a large display.

The Big Picture: Where is everybody?

A. Listen to the conversation between Tommy and his mother.

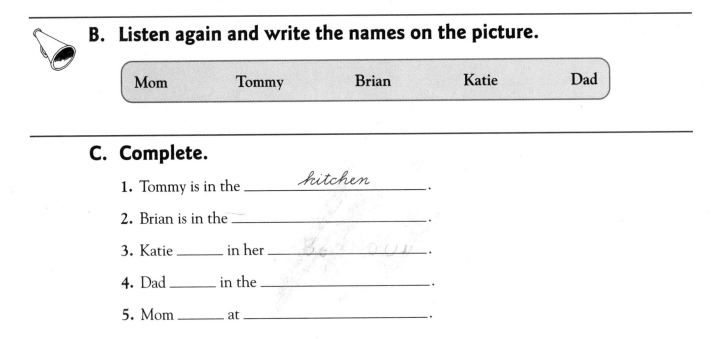

B. Listen again and write the names on the picture.

Mom	Tommy	Brian	Katie	Dad

C. Complete.

1. Tommy is in the _____ kitchen _____.

2. Brian is in the _____.

3. Katie _____ in her _____ Be____ _____.

4. Dad _____ in the _____.

5. Mom _____ at _____.

D. Listen and circle.

1. **a.** She's at work.   *(circled)*   **b.** She's talking on the telephone.
2. **a.** He's in the kitchen.   **b.** He's talking on the telephone.
3. **a.** He's in the kitchen. *(circled)*   **b.** He's talking on the telephone. *(circled)*
4. **a.** She's in her bedroom.   **b.** She's talking on the telephone.
5. **a.** She's in her bedroom.   **b.** She's talking on the telephone. *(circled)*
6. **a.** He's in the living room. *(circled)*   **b.** He's sleeping.
7. **a.** He's in the living room.   **b.** He's sleeping. *(circled)*

E. Listen and write.

1. _____ *No, she isn't.* _____
2. _____
3. _____
4. _____
5. _____
6. _____
7. _____
8. _____

Yes, he is.
No, he isn't.

Yes, she is.
No, she isn't.

F. Answer.

1. Where is Tommy? _____ *He's in the kitchen.* _____

2. Is he playing video games? _____

3. What's he doing? _____

4. Where is Katie? _____

5. What's she doing? _____

6. Is she doing her homework? _____

G. Write a story about this family.

A. Complete.

1. Put the _____table_____ in the _____dining room_____ .

2. Put the _____ in the _____ .

3. Put the _____ in the _____ .

4. Put the _____ .

5. Put the _____ .

6. _____ .

B. Answer.

1. Where is he? _____He's in the kitchen._____

2. What is he doing? _____

3. Is he cooking dinner? _____

4. Where is he? _____

5. What is he doing? _____

6. Is he watching TV? _____

7. Where are you? _____

8. What are you doing? _____

9. Are you watching TV?   Yes, I am.   No, I'm not.

10. Are you doing your homework?   Yes, I am.   No, I'm not.

A. Read.

I live in a large building on Houston Street. The apartment is on the third floor. The apartment has three rooms, and they are very large. My mom and dad have the bedroom. My sister and I sleep in the living room on a pull-out sofa. The TV is in the living room. Sometimes my parents think we are sleeping. We are really watching TV.

I rent a room in a house. My family is in Poland, and I live alone. I work all day. I go to school at night. I don't want an apartment. I don't need a kitchen. I only eat breakfast at home. There is a small refrigerator and a microwave in the room.

I live in a house in San Diego. It's all on one floor. The house has seven rooms. There are three bedrooms and two bathrooms. There is a family room, too. There is a TV and a computer in the family room. We need a large house. I have three children, and my mother lives with us.

B. Check (✓) the sentences that are true for you.

_____ I live in a house.

_____ I live in an apartment.

_____ I live alone.

_____ I live with _____.

_____ There are _____ rooms.

_____ I have a large _____.

_____ I have a small _____.

_____ The TV is in the living room.

_____ There's a TV in my bedroom.

C. Write about your home. Use the sentences above to help you.

> *Writing Note*
> **After you finish, check your spelling.**

Looking at Forms

A. Complete this change-of-address form.

Please send mail to my new address beginning _____ / _____ / _____

                                                     Month   Date   Year

My Name (Last name, first name, middle)

Old Street Address

City   State   Zip Code

New Street Address

City   State   Zip Code

Signature

Culture Note
You can get an official change-of-address form at the post office.

B. Complete this information about your local post office.

My Community

The post office is on _____ .
                                       (street)

It's open from _____ to _____ .

A first-class stamp is $_____ .

It costs $_____ to send a letter to my country.

I. *Have / Need*

I **have** a TV.   I **don't have** a TV.

I **need** a microwave.   I **don't need** a microwave.

2. **Present continuous statements**

I **am** studying.   I**'m** studying.

He **is** sleeping.   He**'s** sleeping.

She **is** eating.   She**'s** eating.

They **are** watching TV.   They**'re** watching TV.

3. *Yes/No questions*

Are you **watching** TV?   Yes, I **am.**   No, I**'m not.**

Is she **watching** TV?   Yes, she **is.**   No, she **isn't.**

Is he **watching** TV?   Yes, he **is.**   No, he **isn't.**

4. *Wh-* **questions**

Where **is** he?   He**'s** in the bedroom.

What**'s** he **doing**?   He**'s reading**.

Dictionary: Places

A. Listen and repeat.

Stores

bank

bakery

bookstore

coffee shop

Laundromat

shoe store

supermarket

drugstore

Places downtown

City Hall

library

police station

park

post office

hospital

parking lot

Dictionary: Prepositions

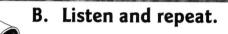

B. Listen and repeat.

The bank is **on the corner of** First Street and Main Street.

Mr. Garcia is standing **in front of** the bank.

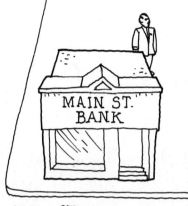

Mr. Garcia is standing **behind** the bank.

Mr. Garcia is standing **next to** the bank.

Mr. Garcia is standing **across from** the bank.

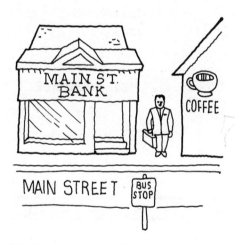

Mr. Garcia is standing **between** the bank and the coffee shop.

61

Grammar in Action
Where's the bank?

A. Listen and complete.

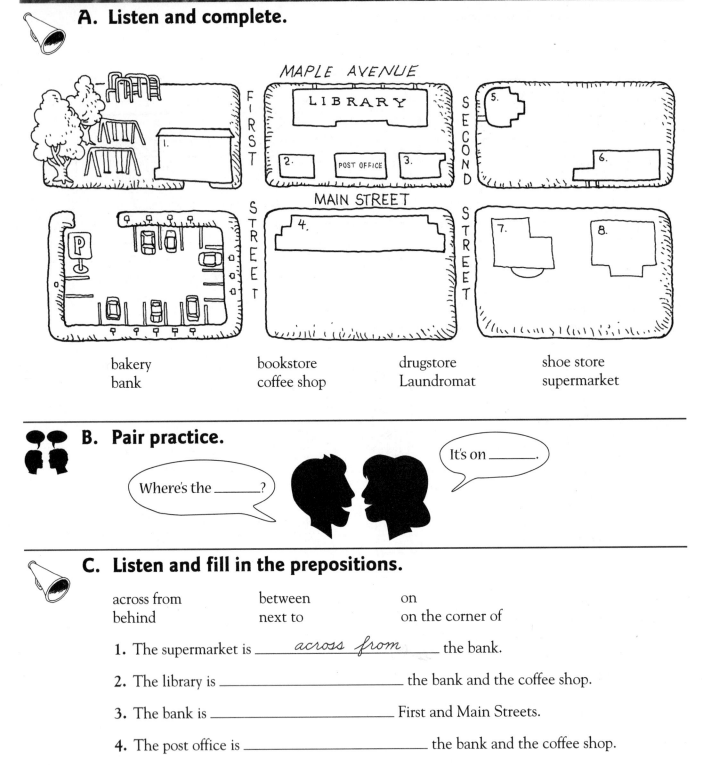

bakery
bank

bookstore
coffee shop

drugstore
Laundromat

shoe store
supermarket

B. Pair practice.

Where's the _____?

It's on _____.

C. Listen and fill in the prepositions.

across from   between   on
behind   next to   on the corner of

1. The supermarket is _____ *across from* _____ the bank.

2. The library is _____ the bank and the coffee shop.

3. The bank is _____ First and Main Streets.

4. The post office is _____ the bank and the coffee shop.

5. The bakery is _____ the park.

6. The Laundromat is _____ Second Street.

7. The bakery is _____ the parking lot.

8. The bookstore is _____ Main Street and Second Street.

Reading a Map

A. Talk about the map.

Examples: The bookstore is next to the bakery.
The parking lot is behind the school.

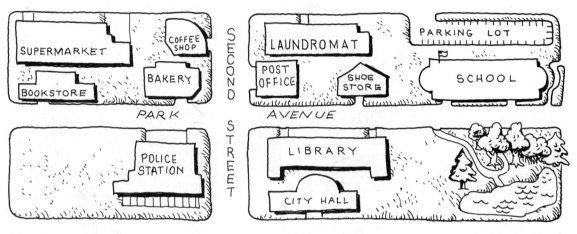

B. Circle Yes or No.

Yes   No   **1.** The coffee shop is next to the post office.

Yes   No   **2.** The park is across from the school.

Yes   No   **3.** The bakery is on the corner of Park Avenue and Second Street.

Yes   No   **4.** City Hall is across from the library.

Yes   No   **5.** The library is on Park Avenue.

Yes   No   **6.** The shoe store is between the school and the post office.

C. Write new sentences about the map.

1. _____

2. _____

3. _____

4. _____

5. _____

> *Writing Note*
> **A street name begins with a capital letter.**

The Public Library

🗣️ **A. Pair practice.** *Ask and answer questions about the library.*

They are = They're

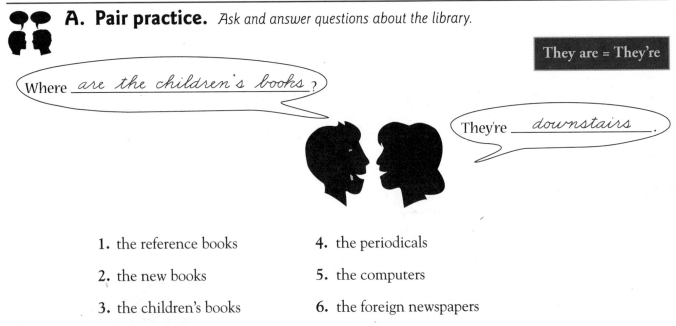

Where *are the children's books* ?

They're *downstairs* .

1. the reference books
2. the new books
3. the children's books

4. the periodicals
5. the computers
6. the foreign newspapers

Working Together: Our Community

A. Complete these sentences about places in your community.

1. The library is on _A ve_ .

2. The telephone number of the library is _914) 335-9821_ .

3. I **have / don't have** a library card.

4. The hospital is on _____ .

5. The telephone number of the hospital is _____ .

6. The police station is on _____ .

7. The telephone number of the police station is _____ .

> *Culture Note*
> For an emergency,
> call 911.

B. Complete.

1. My school is in _N ll Rochelle_ .
   (city)

2. My school is on _____ .
   (street)

3. My school is next to _____ .
   (building)

4. My school is across from _Wanchi_ .
   (building or other location)

C. Write two sentences about the location of your school.

1. _____

2. _____

The Big Picture: Downtown

A. Listen to the story.

B. Listen and circle.

1. **a.** Elena is. **b.** Jane is. **c.** Mrs. Lee is.

2. **a.** Michael is. **b.** Luisa is. **c.** Michael and Luisa are.

3. **a.** Officer Ortiz is. **b.** Mr. Thomas is. **c.** Mark is.

4. **a.** Officer Ortiz is. **b.** Jane is. **c.** Mrs. Lee is.

5. **a.** Mark is. **b.** Joseph is. **c.** Jane is.

6. **a.** Joseph is. **b.** Jane is. **c.** Luisa is.

7. **a.** Joseph and Jane are. **b.** Michael and Luisa are. **c.** Officer Ortiz is.

8. **a.** Mr. Thomas is. **b.** Mrs. Lee is. **c.** Officer Ortiz is.

C. Circle and complete.

1. The playground is _____ Smith Street.
   a. across from   **(b.)** on   c. between

2. City Hall is _____ the playground.
   a. across from   b. next to   c. on the corner of

3. The coffee shop is _____ the bakery.
   a. next to   b. between   c. behind

4. The parking lot is _____ the bakery.
   a. across from   b. behind   c. between

5. Jane and Joseph are sitting _____ the coffee shop.
   a. behind   **b. (in front of)**   c. next to

6. The police station is _____ City Hall.
   a. across from   b. on the corner of   c. on

7. Officer Ortiz is standing _____ Mrs. Lee's car.
   a. next to   b. behind   c. on

8. Michael and Luisa are _____ City Hall.
   a. behind   b. in front of   c. across from

D. Complete.

1. _____*City Hall*_____ is across from the police station.

2. _____ is behind the bookstore.

3. _____ is next to the coffee shop.

4. _____ is behind the coffee shop.

5. Officer Ortiz is standing between _____ and the bookstore.

6. _____ is on the corner of North Main Street and Smith Street.

E. Listen and write.

He	is	talking.
She		
They	are	

1. Mr. Thomas ____*is*____ ____*talking*____ to the other driver.

2. Elena _____ _____ the children.

3. The children _____ _____.

4. They _____ _____ a good time.

get	sit
have	✓ talk
play	watch
read	work

5. Joseph and Jane _____ _____ at tables.

6. Joseph _____ _____ a newspaper.

7. Mark _____ _____ at the coffee shop.

8. Michael and Luisa _____ _____ married.

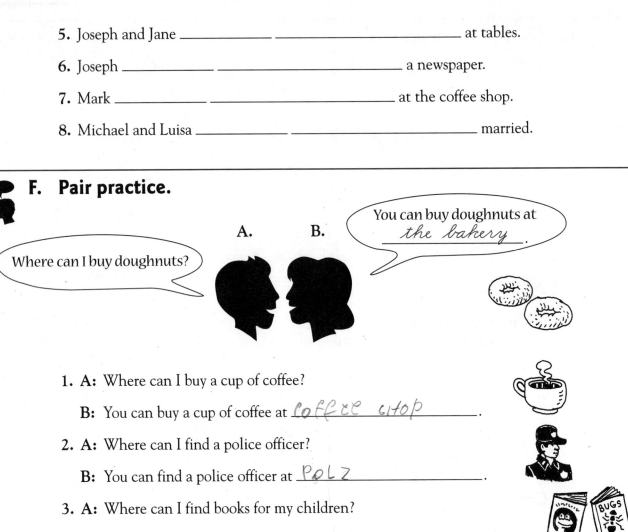

F. Pair practice.

A.   B.

You can buy doughnuts at *the bakery* .

Where can I buy doughnuts?

1. **A:** Where can I buy a cup of coffee?

   B: You can buy a cup of coffee at _coffee shop_ .

2. **A:** Where can I find a police officer?

   B: You can find a police officer at _Polz_ .

3. **A:** Where can I find books for my children?

   B: You can find books for your children at _____ .

4. **A:** Where can I wash my clothes?

   B: You can wash your clothes at _____ .

5. **A:** Where can I buy stamps?

   B: You can buy stamps at _____ .

A. Look at the map. Complete.

1. Where _____ *is* _____ the bank?

   It's _____ the bakery.

2. Where _____ *is School* _____ the school?

   It's _____ the park.

3. Where _____ *dp* _____ the children?

   They _____ in the _____.

4. What _____ *eh* _____ doing?

   They _____.

5. Where _____ ?

   _____.

6. Where _____ *the* _____ ?

   _____.

7. Where _____ *We City Hall the* _____ ?

   _____.

8. What _____ ?

   _____.

A. Read.

Every Saturday morning, my son and I go to the public library. The library is downtown across from the post office. We can walk there.

My son and I have library cards. We go to the children's section, and he takes out books and videos about animals. He can borrow books for two weeks, but he can only borrow a video for three days.

Story Time is at 10:00. He stays downstairs, and I go upstairs. There's an English class on Saturday mornings. I study English there.

Next to the reference desk, there is a foreign magazine and newspaper section. Every Saturday, I read a magazine or a newspaper from my country.

The library is a wonderful place for both me and my son. And best of all, it's free!

B. Write. *Go to your public library. Sit at a table. What do you see? What are people doing?*

The public library in _____ is on _____ .
(town or city)   (street)

It is open _____ days a week. On Saturday, it is open from
(number)

_____ *to* _____ .
(opening time)   (closing time)

I am at the library now. _____

When adv. cuándo conj. cuando

Which   *Whos*

HOW

Wehere   What

> *Writing Note*
> **After you finish, check your punctuation.**

Looking at Forms: Library Card Application

A. Complete.

Public Library Card Application

_____ _____ _____ ___/___/___
(Last Name)   First Name   MI   Today's Date

☐ Adult ☐ Child _____-____-_____ _____
                          Social Security Number   (If child, Signature of Parent/Guardian)

_____
Address

_____ _____ _____
City   State   Zip Code

Telephone: (   ) _____

71

Summary

1. Prepositions

Where is the library?   It is **on** Maple Avenue.

Where are the foreign newspapers?   They are **next to** the computers.

2. *Who* Questions

Who is watching the children?   Elena is.

Who is drinking coffee?   Joseph and Jane are.

> *Note*
> <u>Who</u> takes a singular verb in the question form.

3. Where can I . . .?

Where can I buy stamps?   **You can buy** stamps at the post office.

Where can I find a police officer?   **You can find** a police officer at the police station.

Dictionary

A. Listen and repeat.

Jobs

beautician
A beautician cuts hair.

manicurist
A manicurist colors nails.

cashier
A cashier takes money.

security guard
A security guard watches customers.

cook
A cook prepares food.

waiter
A waiter takes orders.

salesperson
A salesperson helps customers.

pharmacist
A pharmacist fills prescriptions.

photographer
A photographer takes pictures.

74

florist
A florist sells flowers.

painter
A painter paints walls and ceilings.

custodian
A custodian sweeps floors.

Grammar in Action
Where does he work?

75

A. Listen and write the job.

1. He's a _____ waiter _____.
2. She's a _____ manicurist _____.
3. She's a _____ beautician _____.
4. He's a _____ cashier _____.
5. He's a _____ pharmacist _____.
6. She's a _____ custodian _____.
7. He's a _____ securiti guard _____.

pharmacist
✓ custodian
✓ waiter
cashier
✓ manicurist
security guard
✓ beautician

What does he do?

B. Pair practice. *Talk about the jobs in the mall.*

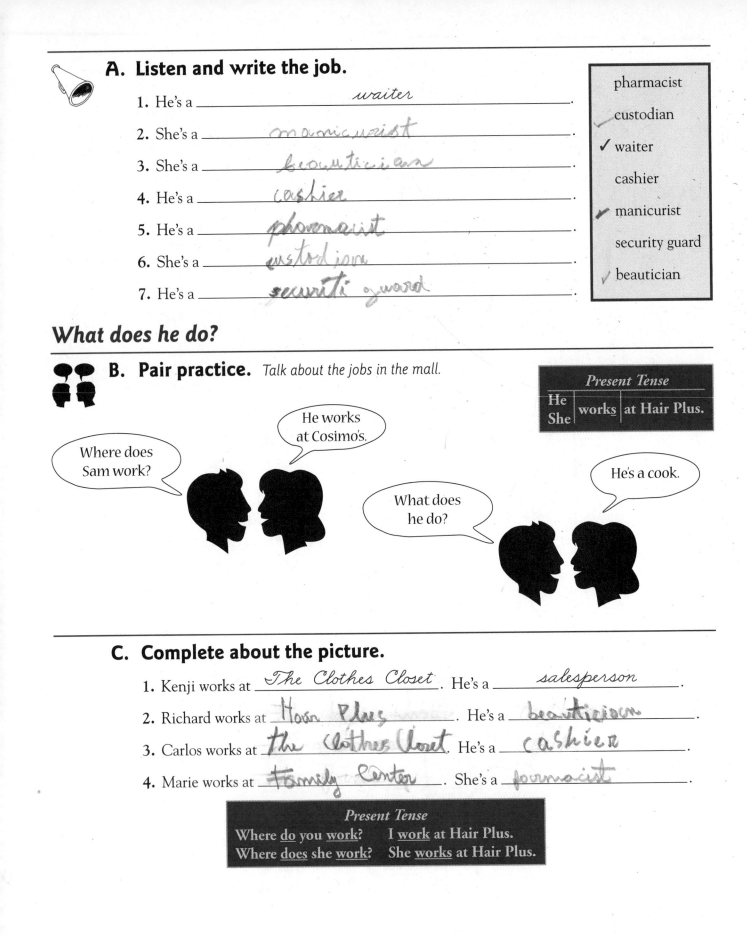

Where does Sam work?

He works at Cosimo's.

What does he do?

He's a cook.

Present Tense		
He She	works	at Hair Plus.

C. Complete about the picture.

1. Kenji works at _____ The Clothes Closet _____. He's a _____ salesperson _____.
2. Richard works at _____ Hair Plus _____. He's a _____ beautician _____.
3. Carlos works at _____ the Clothes Closet _____. He's a _____ cashier _____.
4. Marie works at _____ Family Center _____. She's a _____ pharmacist _____.

Present Tense	
Where **do** you **work**?	I **work** at Hair Plus.
Where **does** she **work**?	She **works** at Hair Plus.

76

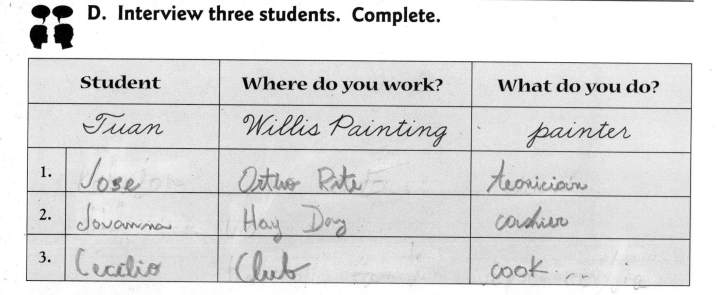

D. Interview three students. Complete.

Student	Where do you work?	What do you do?
Tuan	*Willis Painting*	*painter*
1. *Jose*	*Ortho Rite*	*teonician*
2. *Jovanna*	*Hay Day*	*cashier*
3. *Cecilio*	*Club*	*cook*

E. Complete.

1. ___*Tuan*___ works at ___*Willis Painting*___. ___*He*___ is a ___*painter*___.
   (name)   (place)   (He/She)   (job)

2. ___*Betty*___ works at ___*house cleaning*___. ___*She*___ is a ___c___.
   (name)   (place)   (He/She)   (job)

3. _____ works at _____. _____ is a _____.
   (name)   (place)   (He/She)   (job)

What do you do there?

A. Complete.

1. A beautician ___*cuts*___ hair.

2. A custodian ___*sweeps*___ the floor.

3. A security guard ___*watches*___ customers.

4. A florist ___*sells*___ flowers.

5. A cook ___*prepares*___ food.

6. A manicurist ___*color*___ nails.

7. A pharmacist ___*fills*___ prescriptions.

8. A photographer ___*takes*___ pictures.

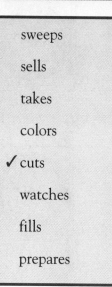

sweeps

sells

takes

colors

✓ cuts

watches

fills

prepares

B. Listen and match.

A

B

C

D

Conversation 1: _____

Conversation 2: _____

Conversation 3: _____

Conversation 4: _____

C. Write about your job experience.

| I **am** = now |
| I **was** = in the past |

1. Where do you work? I work at _Scardale_ .

2. What do you do? I'm a _babisister_ .

3. What do you do there? I _care a baby_ . I _____ .

4. In my country, I was a _nurse_ .

5. In the future, I'd like to be a _nurse_ .

D. Read your sentences to a partner.

What time is it?

A. Listen and repeat.

two o'clock
2:00

two oh-five
2:05

two ten
2:10

two fifteen
2:15

two thirty
2:30

two forty
2:40

two forty-five
2:45

two fifty
2:50

two fifty-five
2:55

three o'clock
3:00

B. Show the time on the clocks. Say the time.

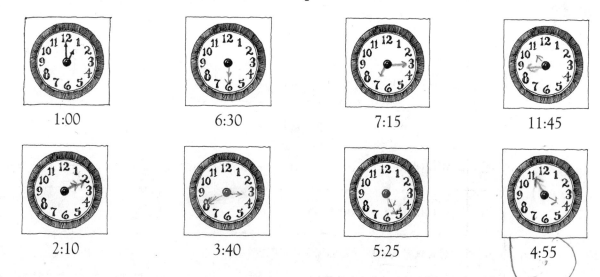

1:00   6:30   7:15   11:45

2:10   3:40   5:25   4:55

C. Listen and show the time on the clocks.

A   B   C   D

2:50   7:45   10:00   12:55

What time do you get up?

Present Tense		
I	get up	at 7:00.
He	gets up	

A. Read. Complete the time.

Amit gets up at 7:00.
I get up at _8:00_

Amit eats breakfast at 7:30.
I eat breakfast at _8_:_30_

Amit leaves home at 8:00.
I leave home at _9:00_

Amit works from 9:00 to 5:00.
I work from _10:00_ to _4:00_

Amit studies from 7:30 to 9:00.
I study from _7:00_ to _9:00_

Amit goes to bed at 12:00.
I go to bed at _11:00_

Prepositions
I get <u>to</u> school <u>at</u> 7:20.   I study <u>from</u> 7:30 <u>to</u> 9:00.

79

B. Pair practice. *Sit with a partner. Ask the questions and complete the times.*

		Me	**My Partner**
1.	What time do you get up?	9:00	6:45
2.	What time do you eat breakfast?		
3.	What time do you leave your home?		
4.	What time do you work?		
5.	What time do you study?		
6.	What time do you go to bed?		

in the morning

in the afternoon

in the evening

at night

Work Schedules

A. Listen and repeat.

Writing Note
The days of the week begin with capital letters.

Sunday	Monday	Tuesday	Wednesday	Thursday	Friday	Saturday

Saturday and Sunday = the weekend

B. Read the schedule. Answer the questions.

Hair Plus				
	Richard	Sheri	Bob	Olga
Tuesday	10-6	10-6	off	3-6
Wednesday	10-6	off	10-6	off
Thursday	10-6	3-6	3-6	off
Friday	10-6	10-6	3-6	10-6
Saturday	10-6	10-6	10-6	10-6

1. Who works five days a week? _____ Richard _____ does.
2. Who works full time? _____ Richard _____ does.
3. Who works part time? _____ Olga _____ does.
4. What days does Olga work? _____ Tuesday, Friday, Saturday _____
5. What days does Sheri work? _____ Tuesday, Thursday, Friday, Saturday _____
6. How many hours a week does Richard work? _____ 40 _____
7. How many hours a week does Bob work? _____ 3456 _____
8. What days does Olga have off? _____ Wednesday, Thursday _____

> Full time = 40 hours a week
> Part time = less than 40 hours a week

C. Complete.

1. I work _____.
   full time/part time

2. I work __3__ hours a day.

3. I work _____ days a week.

4. I work _____ hours a week.

5. I work _____.
   (Sunday   Monday   Tuesday   Wednesday   Thursday   Friday   Saturday)

6. I have _____ off.
   (Sunday   Monday   Tuesday   Wednesday   Thursday   Friday   Saturday)

D. Read your sentences to a partner.

Working Together

A. Laura's Day

Laura has a busy day. She works full time, and she goes to school. Sit with a partner. Put her schedule in order from 1 to 10.

watches TV ◯   gets up ①.   studies ②   eats dinner ③

reads the newspaper ⑥   eats breakfast ⑦

takes a walk ⑤   takes a shower ④   goes to bed ⑧   works ⑨

B. Write a story about Laura's day.

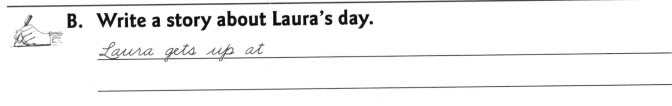

Laura gets up at _____

_____

_____

_____

_____

_____

_____

82

A. Read.

Stuart is a security guard at Parkside Mall. He works full time. He works 40 hours a week, from Wednesday to Sunday. His hours are from 1:00 PM to 9:00 PM. Stuart walks up and down the mall all day. He answers questions, and he gives directions. Stuart carries a cell phone. In an emergency, he calls the police or an ambulance. Stuart likes his job.

B. Write about your job.

I am a _____. I work at _____. It's
     (job)   (company)

in _____, on _____. I work
  (city)   (street)

_____. I work _____ hours a week. _____
(full time / part time)

_____

_____

_____

_____

_____

Writing Note
Always check your spelling.

83

The Big Picture: The CD Den

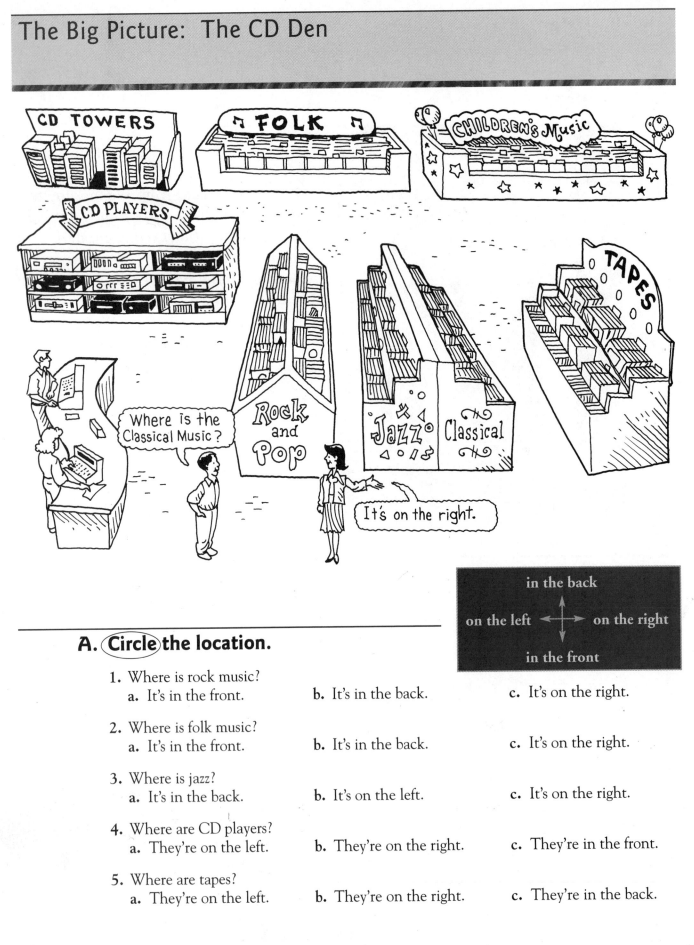

A. Circle the location.

	in the back
on the left ←→	on the right
	in the front

1. Where is rock music?
   a. It's in the front.   **b.** It's in the back.   **c.** It's on the right.

2. Where is folk music?
   a. It's in the front.   **b.** It's in the back.   **c.** It's on the right.

3. Where is jazz?
   a. It's in the back.   **b.** It's on the left.   **c.** It's on the right.

4. Where are CD players?
   a. They're on the left.   **b.** They're on the right.   **c.** They're in the front.

5. Where are tapes?
   a. They're on the left.   **b.** They're on the right.   **c.** They're in the back.

Listen. Then complete.

manager	security guard	Sunday
employees	assistant manager	part time
full time	✓ music	Saturday

1. The CD Den is a _____music_____ store.

2. Eric is the _____music_____ of the CD Den.

3. Eric works _____fullay_____, about fifty hours a week.

4. Mei-Lin, the _____, works about fifty hours a week, too.

5. There are about 10 other _____CD_____ at CD Den.

6. They all work _____saturday_____, about fifteen to twenty hours a week.

7. The busiest days of the week are _____ and _____.

8. On weekends, there is a _____.

> employer = owner, company
> employee = worker

C. Listen. Write the day and times.

1. James can work _____Monday_____ from _5_ : _00_ to _9_ : _00_.

2. Gloria can work _____ from _12_ : _8_ to ___ : ___.

3. Makiko can work _____ from _1_ : ___ to ___ : ___.

4. Andre can work on _____ from ___ : ___ to ___ : ___.

5. Lucy can work _____ from _3_ : _5_ to ___ : ___.

D. Listen and answer.

Schedule	
James	Lucy
Saturday	Monday
10-6	5-10
Sunday	Tuesday
10-6	5-10
Wednesday	Friday
5-9	5-10

1. _____Yes, he does._____

2. _____

3. _____

4. _____Wednesday_____

5. _____

6. _____

> Yes, he does.
> No, he doesn't.

> Yes, she does.
> No, she doesn't.

E. Sit with a partner. Write a story about the CD Den.

A. What time is it?

It's __3__ .   It's __5:12__ .   It's __8__ .   It's _____ .

B. Write the answer.

No, she works part time.	✓ She's a manicurist.
She works four days a week.	She works from 10:00 to 6:00.
Yes, she does.	She works at Hair Plus.
She was a beautician.	

1. What does Sheri do? ___*She's a manicurist.*___

2. Where does she work? _____

3. How many days does she work? _____

4. Does she work full time? _____

5. What hours does she work? _____

6. Does she like her job? _____

7. What was her job in her country? _____

C. Complete. Write *at, from,* or *to.*

at	*from/to*
at 10:00	from 10:00 to 6:00

Eric gets up ____*at*____ 8:00. He takes a shower and has a small breakfast, and then he drives to work. Eric arrives at work _____ 9:45, before the store opens. _____ 10:00, he unlocks the store. Eric works _____ 10:00 _____ 6:00 six days a week. Two nights a week, Eric goes to school _____ 7:00 _____ 10:00. He's studying for a degree in business. Eric is a night person. He studies or watches TV _____ 10:00 _____ 12:00. He goes to bed _____ 12:30.

Looking at Forms: A Work Application

A. Complete.

The CD Den

Name: _____
    (First)   (Last)   (Middle Initial)

Address: _____
                              (Street)

_____
    (City)   (Zip Code)

Telephone Number: (_____)_____

Social Security Number: _____

I can work _____ hours a week.

I can work (circle): Sunday Monday Tuesday Wednesday Thursday Friday Saturday

I can work from _____:_____ to _____:_____.

Summary

1. Present tense

I **work** at Hair Plus.

He **works** at Hair Plus.

She **works** at Hair Plus.

2. Yes/No questions

Does he **work** at Hair Plus?	Yes, he **does.**	No, he **doesn't.**
Do you **work** at Hair Plus?	Yes, I **do.**	No, I **don't.**

3. Wh-questions

Where **does** he **work?**	He works at Cosimo's.
What **does** he **do?**	He's a waiter.
What **does** he **do** there?	He takes people's orders.
What hours **does** he **work?**	He works from 5:00 to 10:00.

4. Prepositions: *at, from/to*

She gets up **at** 7:00.

She goes **to** school **from** 8:00 **to** 3:00.

Dictionary

 A. Listen and repeat.

Coins

a penny
one cent
$ .01

a nickel
five cents
$ .05

a dime
ten cents
$ .10

a quarter
twenty-five cents
$ .25

> *Culture Note*
> From 1999 to 2009, the United States is issuing a new series of quarters. The quarters will honor the different states. Do you have any of these new quarters? What state is on the back?

Bills

a dollar
$1.00

five dollars
$5.00

ten dollars
$10.00

twenty dollars
$20.00

Kitchen items

pot

pan

wok

microwave

rice cooker

toaster oven

can opener

teakettle

coffeemaker

mugs

glasses

pot holders

dishes

spoons

knives

forks

Grammar in Action

Coins

A. Listen and repeat.

a. 4¢ $ .04

b. 10¢ $ .10

c. 25¢ $ .25

d. 30¢ $ .30

e. 35¢ $ .35

f. 50¢ $ .50

g. 62¢ $ .62

h. 75¢ $ .75

i. 85¢ $ .85

j. 99¢ $ .99

> *Money Note*
> There are two ways
> to write cents.
> **Example: ten cents**
> 10¢
> $ .10

B. Pair practice. *Say the amounts above with a partner.*

C. Write the amount.

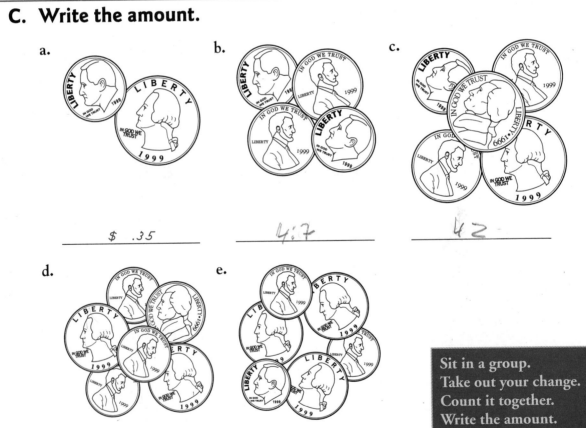

a. ____ $ .35 ____

b. ____ 4:7 ____

c. ____ 42 ____

d. ____

e. ____

> Sit in a group.
> Take out your change.
> Count it together.
> Write the amount.
> Who has the most change?

D. Listen and write the amount.

a. _____$ .02_____   d. _____   g. _____

b. _____   e. _____   h. _____

c. _____   f. _____   i. _____

Bills

> ### Dollars and Cents
> $ 2.50 - two <u>dollars</u> and fifty <u>cents</u> *or*
> two fifty
> $10.99 - ten <u>dollars</u> and ninety-nine <u>cents</u> *or*
> ten ninety-nine

A. Listen and repeat.

a. $1.00	d. $4.99	g. $12.98
b. $1.50	e. $7.37	h. $24.95
c. $2.75	f. $9.85	i. $77.20

B. Pair practice. *Say the amounts with a partner.*

C. Listen and write the amount.

a. _____$1.00_____   d. _____   g. _____

b. _____   e. _____   h. _____

c. _____   f. _____   i. _____

D. Write the amount.

a. $ 2.20 *two dollars and twenty cents* _____

b. $ 3.50 _____

c. $ 9.95 _____

d. $15.50 _____

e. $25.60 _____

f. $47.35 _____

g. $79.43 _____

How much is it?

A. Write the name of each item.

teakettle	wok	coffeemaker
pot	microwave	rice cooker

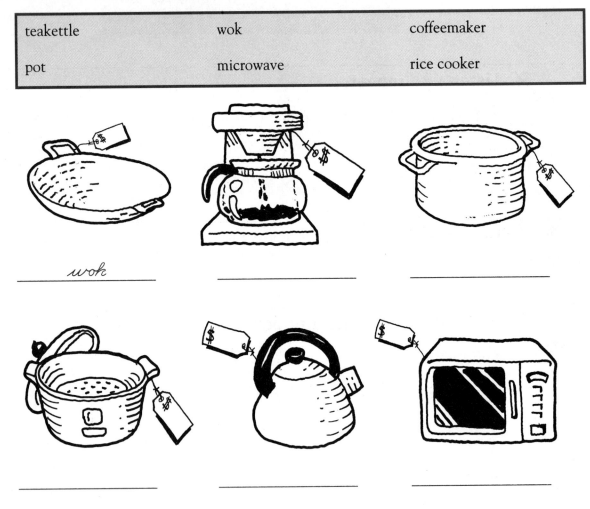

wok _____   _____   _____

_____   _____   _____

 B. Listen and write the price on each item above.

C. Pair practice. *Write the name of each item and a price.*

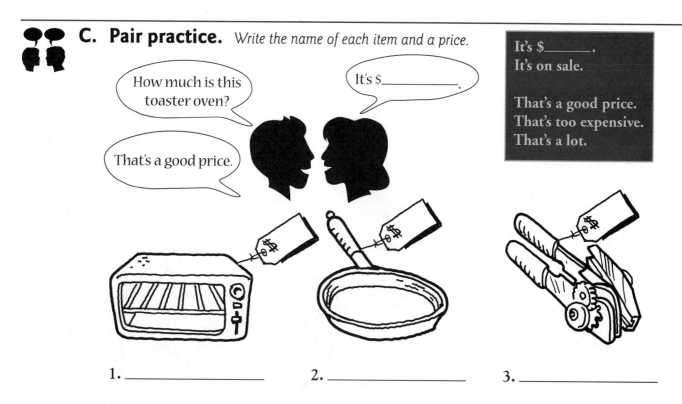

How much is this toaster oven?

That's a good price.

It's $_____.

It's $_____.
It's on sale.

That's a good price.
That's too expensive.
That's a lot.

1. _____

2. _____

3. _____

How much are they?

A. Write the name of each item.

glasses	dishes	mugs
spoons	pot holders	knives

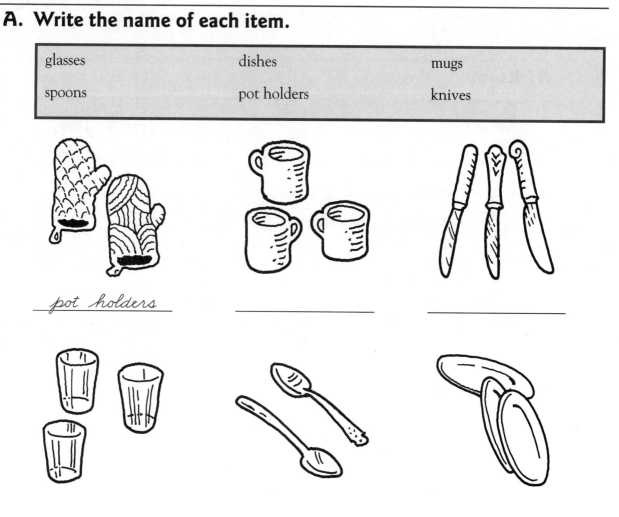

pot holders

_____

_____

_____

_____

_____

B. Listen and write the price on each item in Part A.

C. Pair practice. *Put a price on each item.*

How much are the cups?

That's a good price.

They're
$_____ .

They're $_____ .
They're $_____
each.
They're on sale.
That's a good price.
That's too expensive.
That's a lot.

Checks

A. Read.

	Date ___3/9/0_
Pay to the order of _____City One_____	$ 67.12
sixty-seven 12/00	dollars
First National Bank	
	Juan Hernandez

B. Write these check amounts.

Writing Note
Put the cents amount over /oo.

$ 21.40 *twenty-one 40/00*

$137.95 *one hundred and thirty-seven 95/00*

$359.80 *three hundred and fifty nine 80/00*

a. $ 7.50 _____

b. $ 34.25 _____

c. $ 59.49 _____

d. $137.12 _____

e. $429.67 _____

C. Complete these checks.

| To:
The
Kitchen
Center

$84.95 | Date _____

Pay to the order of _____ $ [   ]

_____ dollars

First National Bank

_____ |

| To:
United
Credit

$237.52 | Date _____

Pay to the order of _____ $ [   ]

_____ dollars

First National Bank

_____ |

Working Together

A. Complete with the name of a store.

1. I shop at _____ for clothes.

2. I shop at _____ for shoes.

3. I shop at _____ for food.

4. I shop at _____ for sports equipment.

5. I shop at _____ for CDs.

6. I shop at _____ for books.

7. I shop at _____ for _____ .

B. Sit in a group of four students. Talk about the places where you like to shop.

C. Sit in a group. Complete.

1. A first-class stamp is _____.

2. A local telephone call is _____.

3. The local newspaper is _____.

4. A gallon of regular gas is _____.

5. A cup of coffee is _____.

6. A CD is _____.

7. A video rental is _____.

8. A ticket at the movie theater is _____.

9. A round-trip airline ticket to my country is _____.

10. A computer is _____.

> **What else is less than $1.00?**

D. Bring in sales circulars from different stores. Sit in a group and discuss.

Where is the sale? Do you shop there?

What kind of store is it? When is the sale?

List four items on sale. What is the regular price? What is the sale price?

E. Complete about two banks in your area.

Bank: _____

Street: _____

The bank is open from _____ to _____ on weekdays.

The bank is open late on _____ night.

The bank is open on Saturday from _____ to _____.

```
Bank: _____

Street: _____

The bank is open from _____ to _____ on weekdays.

The bank is open late on _____ night.

The bank is open on Saturday from _____ to _____.
```

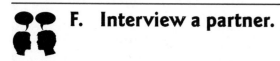 **F. Interview a partner.**

ATM = Automated Teller Machine

How do you pay for	I pay cash.	I use a credit card.	I write a check.	I get a money order.	I use my ATM card.
gas					
rent					
food					
your telephone bill					
your electric bill					
clothes					

G. Put these ATM steps in order.

_____ Select "Withdraw cash."

_____ Take your cash.

___1___ Insert your ATM card.

_____ Take your receipt.

_____ Put in your PIN number.

_____ Remove your ATM card!

_____ Choose the amount you want.

Sharing Our Stories

A. Read.

I save money on food. Four or five supermarkets are near my home. I stop at two or three a week. I buy food on sale. When coffee is on sale, I buy four cans. When spaghetti is on sale, I buy five or six boxes. I use coupons from the newspaper and from the papers that come to my home.

I miss my family so much. I used to spend $100 or more every month calling my sisters and my father. Then I bought a computer. I e-mail my family three or four times a week. Now I just call at special times like birthdays and holidays. I only call late at night and on weekends.

B. Check (✔) the ways you save money. Sit with a partner and compare your lists.

- ☐ I shop at sales.
- ☐ I shop at discount stores.
- ☐ I use coupons.
- ☐ I shop at garage sales.
- ☐ I don't buy lunch. I bring my lunch to work.
- ☐ I don't have a car. I take the bus or walk.
- ☐ I shop on the Internet.
- ☐ I only call my country on weekends.

☐ I use the library.

☐ I tape my favorite songs.

☐ _____

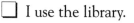 **C. Write a story about one way you try to save money.**

The Big Picture: A Yard Sale

Culture Note
Yard sales are also called
tag sales
garage sales

A. Circle the items that you see at this yard sale.

bed	mirror	pots	dishes	rice cooker
dresser	rug	pans	spoons	toys
table	desk	glasses	forks	teakettle
four chairs	TV	mugs	knives	coffeemaker
lamp	vacuum	toaster oven	wok	microwave

C. Write *is* or *are*. Then put a price.

> *How Much*
> How much <u>is</u> the pot?   It's $4.00.
> How much <u>are</u> the pots?   They're $4.00 each.

1. How much ___*is*___ the wok?   *It's $6.00.*

2. How much ___*are*___ the glasses?   *They're $1.00 each.*

3. How much _____ the dishes?   _____

4. How much _____ the bed?   _____

5. How much _____ the chairs?   _____

6. How much _____ the coffeemaker?   _____

7. How much _____ the lamp?   _____

D. Listen and (circle.) How much are they going to pay?

1. a. $3.00   (b.) $4.00   c. $5.00

2. a. $ .01   b. $ .10   c. $1.00

3. a. $15.00   b. $20.00   c. $25.00

4. a. $ 5.00   b. $ 6.00   c. $ 7.00

5. a. $25.00   b. $30.00   c. $40.00

6. a. $ 1.00   b. $ 2.00   c. $ 3.00

> *Culture Note*
> **You can negotiate the price at a yard sale.**

E. Pair practice. *One student is having a yard sale. The other student is at the yard sale.*
Negotiate a price for these items.

> How much is this coffeemaker?   How much are the mugs?

1.   2.   3.

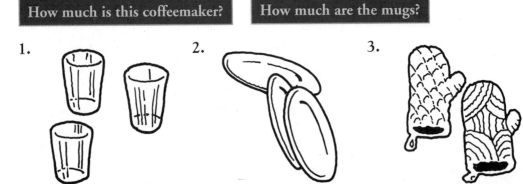

102

> **Dollars and Cents**
> $ 2.50 - two <u>dollars</u> and fifty <u>cents</u> *or* two fifty
> $10.99 - ten <u>dollars</u> and ninety-nine <u>cents</u> *or* ten ninety-nine

A. Write the amount.

a. $ 1.00 *one dollar* _____

b. $ 4.50 _____

c. $ 7.98 _____

d. $ 18.75 _____

e. $ 79.63 _____

f. $135.72 _____

g. $199.00 _____

B. Write the answer.

| It's $_____. | | They're $_____. |

1. How much are the dishes? _____ *They're $29.00.*

2. How much is the microwave? _____

3. How much are mugs? _____

4. How much are the pot holders? _____

103

5. How much is the wok? _____

6. How much is the rice cooker? _____

7. How much are spoons? _____

Looking at Numbers

A. Figure the change.

	Total	Paid	Change
a.	$ .37	$ .50	$ .13
b.	$ .72	$ 1.00	_____
c.	$ 1.75	$ 2.00	_____
d.	$ 4.60	$ 5.00	_____
e.	$ 7.98	$10.00	_____
f.	$15.50	$20.00	_____
g.	$27.35	$30.00	_____
h.	$52.15	$60.00	_____
i.	$67.72	$80.00	_____
j.	$75.98	$100.00	_____

Summary

1. *How much* questions

How much is it?	It's $10.00.
How much is the wok?	It's $10.00.
How much are they?	They're $10.00.
How much are the dishes?	They're $10.00.

2. Dollars and cents

$4.95 – four dollars and ninety-five cents

four ninety-five

3. Writing check amounts

$4.95 – four 95/00

Dictionary

A. Listen and repeat.

For women

blouse

sweater

dress

skirt

bra

underpants

panty hose

For men

tie

shirt

pants

briefs

For both men and women

jacket

belt

jeans

shorts

suit

For the feet

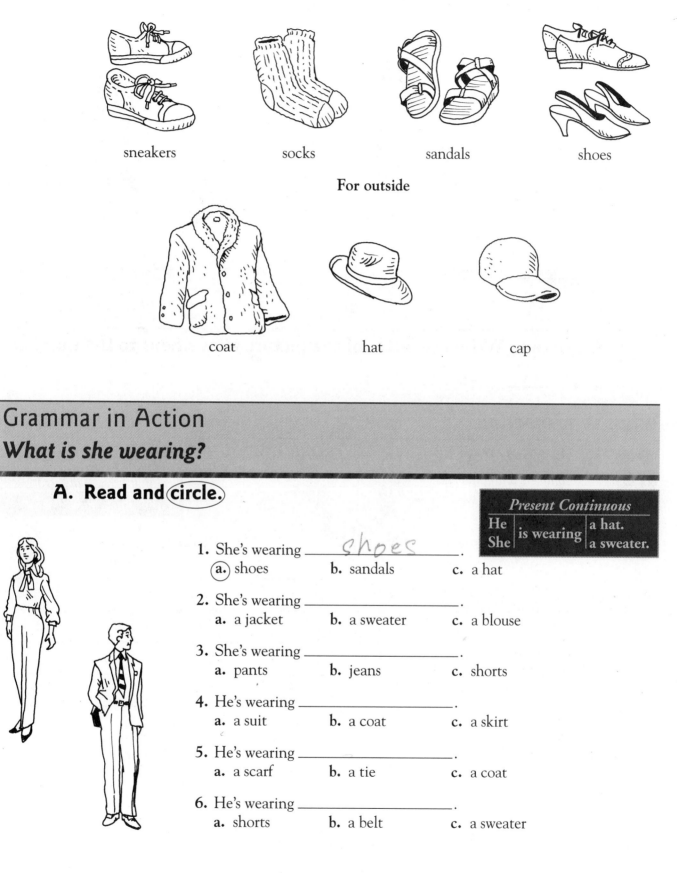

sneakers   socks   sandals   shoes

For outside

coat   hat   cap

Grammar in Action
What is she wearing?

A. Read and (circle.)

Present Continuous		
He	is wearing	a hat.
She		a sweater.

1. She's wearing ___shoes___ .
     a. shoes   **b.** sandals   **c.** a hat

2. She's wearing _____ .
     a. a jacket   **b.** a sweater   **c.** a blouse

3. She's wearing _____ .
     a. pants   **b.** jeans   **c.** shorts

4. He's wearing _____ .
     a. a suit   **b.** a coat   **c.** a skirt

5. He's wearing _____ .
     a. a scarf   **b.** a tie   **c.** a coat

6. He's wearing _____ .
     a. shorts   **b.** a belt   **c.** a sweater

B. Fill in the names of the clothing.

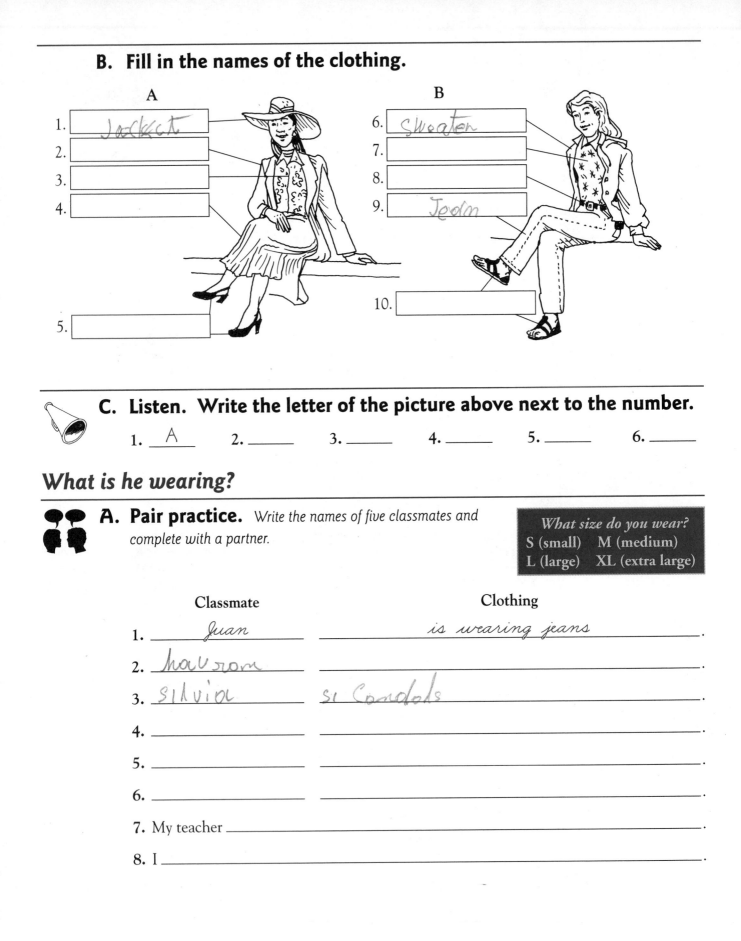

A

1. Jacket
2.
3.
4.
5.

B

6. Sweater
7.
8.
9. Jean
10.

C. Listen. Write the letter of the picture above next to the number.

1. __A__   2. _____   3. _____   4. _____   5. _____   6. _____

What is he wearing?

A. Pair practice. Write the names of five classmates and complete with a partner.

> **What size do you wear?**
> S (small)   M (medium)
> L (large)   XL (extra large)

Classmate	Clothing
1. Juan	is wearing jeans .
2. hausom	.
3. silvia	si Condols .
4.	.
5.	.
6.	.
7. My teacher	.
8. I	.

B. Pair practice. *Put a price on the empty tags.*

| How much | is | the tie? |
| | are | the ties? |

How much is the belt?

It's six dollars and fifty cents.

How much are the shoes?

They're twenty-three dollars.

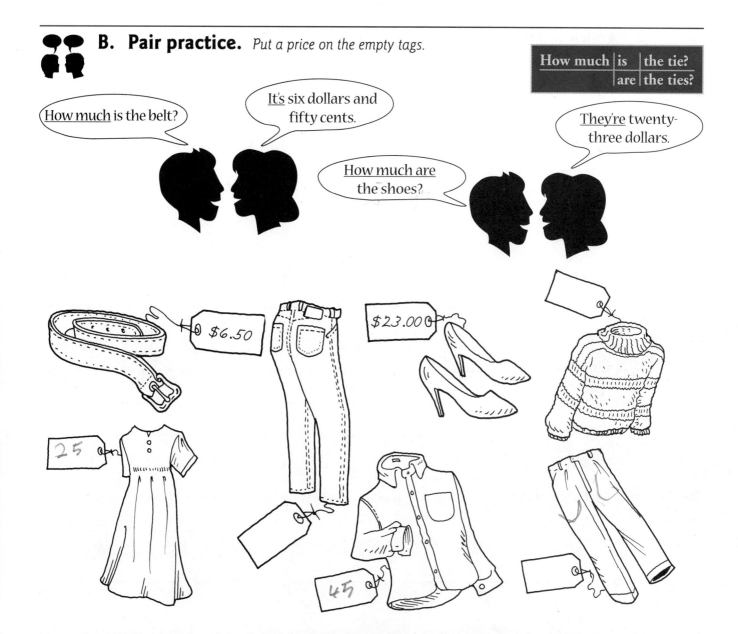

$6.50

$23.00

25

45

Working Together: Buying a Jacket

A. Read and practice.

Clerk: Hello. May I help you?

Customer: Yes, I'm looking for a jacket.

Clerk: What size?

Customer: Medium.

Clerk: What color?

Customer: Brown.

Clerk: Here. Try it on over there in front of the mirror.

Customer: Thank you. It looks good. How much is it?

Clerk: It's $50.00, but today it's on sale for only $35.00.

Customer: Great. I'll take it.

B. Write a conversation between a clerk and a customer. Your teacher will help you.

Clerk: Hello. _____

Customer: Yes, I'm looking for _____

Clerk: _____

Customer: _____

Clerk: _____

Customer: _____

Clerk: Here. _____

Customer: Thank you. It looks _____. How much _____?

Clerk: It's $ _____, but today it's on sale for only $ _____.

Customer: _____. _____

Working Together: At a Sporting Goods Store

A. Label the sports equipment.

basketball	bicycle	soccer ball	weights
baseball bats	bicycle helmet	tennis balls	volleyball
bathing suit	in-line skates	tennis racquets	

bicycle
basketball

tennis
balls

B. Pair practice.

May I help you?

Yes, I play tennis.

I need a new _racquet_.

The tennis raquets are on the wall.

on the left
on the right
on the wall
here
over there

basketball

bathing suit

baseball bat

bicycle helmet

bicycle

soccer ball

volleyball

Using Your English

A. Listen.

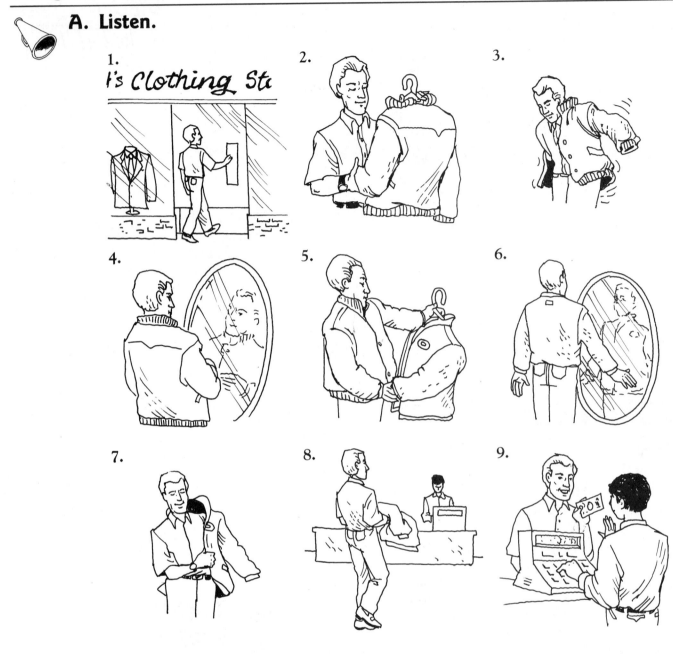

B. Listen and find the picture.

> *Culture Note*
> Save your receipt! You need it if you
> want to return clothing to a store.

C. Listen and repeat.

D. Practice with a partner.

E. Act it out.

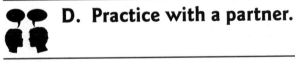

A. Read.

Every summer, my family and I love to go to the beach. We live in California. We are originally from Brazil, and there are many beautiful beaches there, too. The beach in San Diego reminds us of our country.

At the beach, we sit on towels and small chairs under an umbrella. We wear our bathing suits, sunglasses, and hats. We also wear sunblock to protect our skin. We eat fried chicken and fruit and drink lots of juice and water. It's fun to go to the beach.

 B. Write about a place that you like to go with your family in the summer.

Every summer, my family and I like to go to ___bathing___. We live in
(place)

_____. We are originally from _____, and
(state)   (native country)

there are many _____ there, too.
(place–plural)

At the _____, we _____

_____. We wear _____

_____. We eat _____

_____. It's fun to go to _____.

The Big Picture: At the Park

A. Listen.

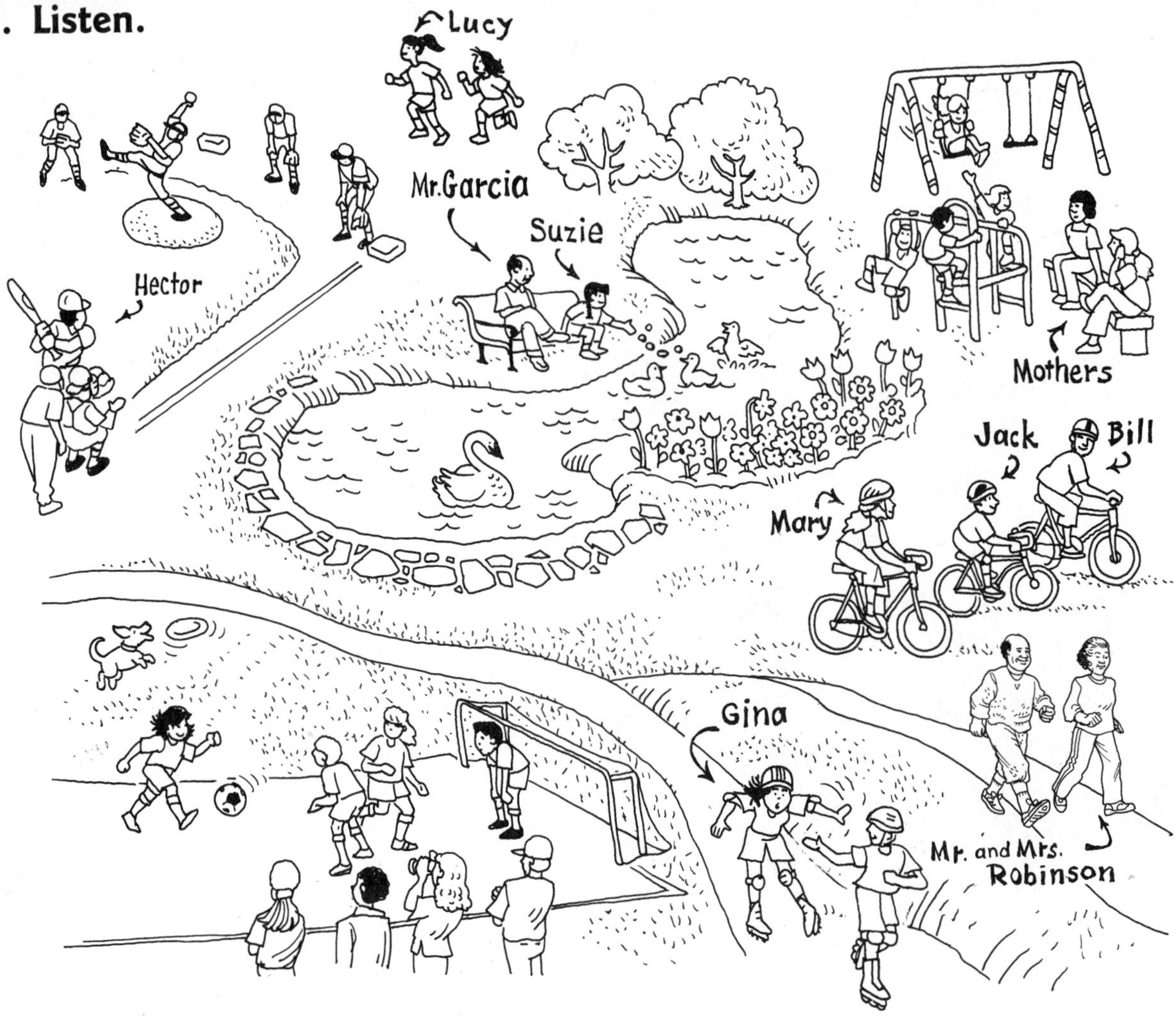

Lucy

Mr. Garcia

Suzie

Hector

Mothers

Jack   Bill

Mary

Gina

Mr. and Mrs. Robinson

B. Listen and circle.

1. (Yes) No   5. Yes No

2. Yes No   6. Yes No

3. Yes No   7. Yes No

4. Yes No   8. Yes No

Culture Note
In many states, the law says, "Children under age 14 must wear helmets."

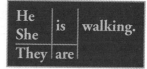

He / She is walking.
They are

C. Listen and circle.

1. **a.** He's playing soccer.   **(b.)** He's playing baseball.   **c.** He's playing volleyball.

2. **a.** Yes, he is.   **b.** No, he isn't.   **c.** Yes, there is.

3. **a.** a uniform.   **b.** a jacket   **c.** a ball

4. **a.** in the pond   **b.** in the park   **c.** in the playground

5. **a.** She's riding a bike.   **b.** She's walking.   **c.** She's in-line skating.

6. **a.** shorts and a T-shirt   **b.** a bathing suit   **c.** a dress

7. **a.** Mr. Garcia is.   **b.** Their parents are.   **c.** The children are.

8. **a.** Hector is.   **b.** Some parents are.   **c.** The children are.

D. Read and complete with *is* or *are* and a verb + *ing*.

feed	help	learn	play	ride	watch	walk

1. Children ____are____ ____playing____ soccer.

2. Their parents _____ _____ the game.

3. Mr. and Mrs. Robinson _____ _____ in the park.

4. Mr. Garcia and his grandaughter _____ _____ the ducks.

5. Jack _____ _____ his bike with his parents.

6. Mothers _____ _____ their children in the playground.

7. Gina _____ _____ to in-line skate.

8. Her boyfriend _____ _____ her.

9. Lucy _____ _____ with her sister, Sally.

E. Write a story about the park.

115

A. Read and answer.

| She | is | wearing | a hat. |
| He | | | jeans. |

What is Gina wearing?

1. She is wearing _____ *a T-shirt* _____ .

2. She is _____ .

3. She _____ .

What is Gina doing?

4. She _____ .

What are Mr. and Mrs. Robinson wearing?

1. Mr. Robinson _____ .

2. He _____ .

3. Mrs. Robinson _____ .

4. She _____ .

What are they doing?

5. They _____ .

B. What do you wear? Read and complete.

1. In the mountains, I wear _____ .

2. At the beach, I wear _____ .

3. At work, I wear _____ .

4. At a party, I wear _____ .

5. On weekends, I wear _____ .

A. Read and figure out.

1. Gina is at the sporting goods store. She's buying a new pair of in-line skates. The skates cost $125.00. Gina is giving the cashier $140.00. What is her change?

Gina's money:	$140.00
Cost of the skates:	$125.00
Gina's change:	$_____.

> *Culture Note*
> The following expressions show cheap prices:
> 1/2 off!   Going Out of Business!   Sale!
> Two for One!   Discount!   Half-Price!

2. Mr. and Mrs. Robinson want to buy a bicycle for their granddaughter's birthday. The bicycle usually costs $100.00, but this week, it's **on sale** for **half-price.** How much is the bicycle?

_____

Summary

1. Present continuous

I **am wearing** a suit.

He **is wearing** a hat.

She **is wearing** shoes.

2. Questions

What **is** he **wearing**?

What **is** she **wearing**?

What **are** you **wearing**?

What **are** they **wearing**?

Contractions

What's he wearing?

What's she wearing?

3. *How much*

How much is the hat?

How much are the shoes?

4. *Wear*

What **do** you **wear** in the winter?

What **do** you **wear** at the beach?

I **wear** a coat and a hat.

I **wear** a bathing suit.

9 Food

Dictionary

A. Listen and repeat.

Breakfast

eggs   toast   cereal   pancakes

bacon   ham   donut

Lunch

hamburger   french fries   salad   soup

turkey sandwich   tuna salad sandwich   lettuce   tomato

Dinner

pasta   chicken   fish

rice   pizza   potatoes

green beans   corn   peas

Beverages

a cup of coffee   a cup of tea   soda   juice   milk

Dessert

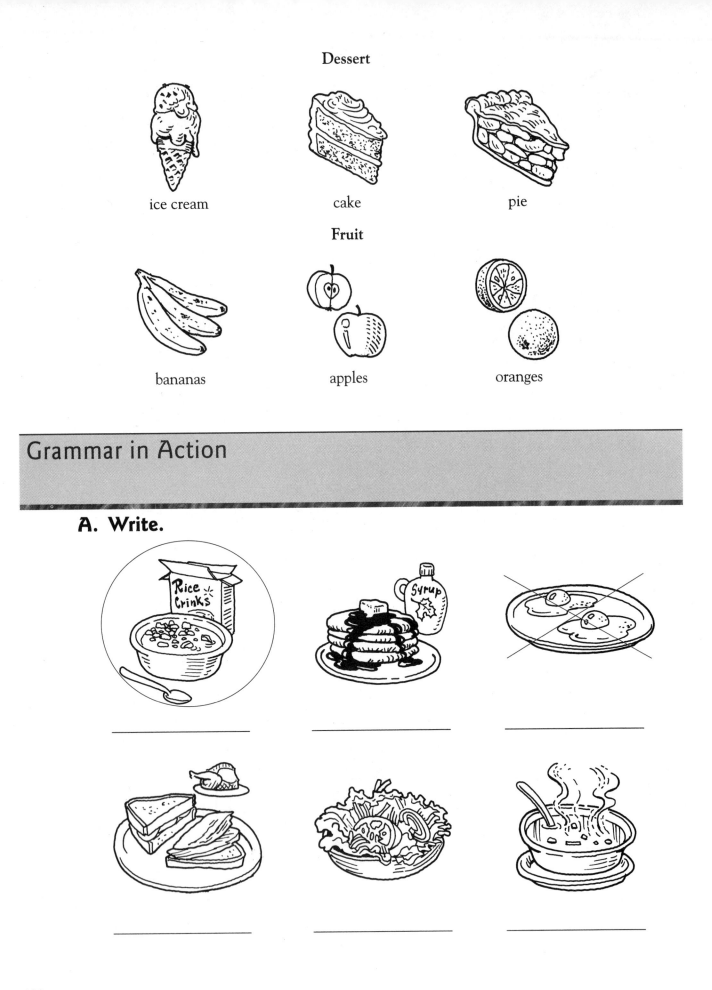

ice cream

cake

pie

Fruit

bananas

apples

oranges

Grammar in Action

A. Write.

_____   _____   _____

 B. Listen and look at Exercise A again. (Circle) the food that Michael likes. C~~ross~~ out the food that he doesn't like.

C. Complete.

| Michael likes _____. |
| Michael **doesn't** like _____. |

| I like _____. |
| I **don't** like _____. |

1. Michael likes ____*cereal*____.

2. He likes _____.

3. Michael doesn't like _____.

4. He doesn't like _____.

5. I like _____.

6. I like _____.

7. I don't like _____.

8. I don't like _____.

What do you eat for breakfast?

A. Complete.

1. What time do you eat breakfast?

   I eat breakfast at _____ : _____ .

2. What do you eat for breakfast?

   I eat _____ and _____ .

3. What time do you eat lunch?

   I eat lunch at _____ : _____ .

| *Culture Note* |
| Americans eat three meals a day. |
| The heaviest meal is dinner. |
| Breakfast |
| Lunch |
| Dinner |

4. What do you eat for lunch?

I eat _____ and _____.

5. What time do you eat dinner?

I eat dinner at _____:_____.

6. What do you eat for dinner?

I eat _____ and _____.

B. Complete with *always, sometimes,* or *never*.

Always	= 100%
Sometimes	= 50%
Never	= 0%

1. I _____ eat breakfast.

2. I _____ drink juice at breakfast.

3. I _____ eat lunch.

4. I _____ eat dinner with my family.

5. I _____ drink coffee at night.

6. I _____ make my own meals.

7. I _____ eat at restaurants.

C. Complete and compare your answers with a partner's.

1. My favorite meal is _____.

2. My favorite drink is _____.

3. My favorite restaurant is _____.

4. My favorite fast-food restaurant is _____.

Ordering Lunch

A. Decide the prices.

Lunch Menu

Sandwiches		Soup	
Tuna salad sandwich	$ 5.95	Vegetable soup	$
Chicken salad sandwich	$	Soup of the day	$
Roast beef sandwich	$		
Turkey sandwich	$	**Beverages**	
Hamburger	$	Coffee, tea	$
Cheeseburger	$	Iced tea	$
Grilled cheese sandwich	$	Soda	$
Salads		**Desserts**	
Chef's salad	$	Ice cream	$
Small salad	$	Cake	$

B. Listen. Number the orders.

_____   _____   1   _____

C. Read and practice.

Waiter:	May I take your order?
Customer:	Yes. A *turkey sandwich* on whole wheat.
Waiter:	Lettuce and tomato?
Customer:	Lettuce. No tomato.
Waiter:	Anything to drink?
Customer:	*Iced tea*, please.

Bread
white
whole wheat
rye
a roll

Working Together

A. Pair practice. *Ask a partner. Check the answer.*

	Yes	No
Do you like hamburgers?		
Do you like turkey sandwiches?		
Do you like french fries?		
Do you like pasta?		
Do you like pizza?		
Do you like ice cream?		

B. Complete about the chart above.

1. I _____ hamburgers.

2. My partner _____ hamburgers.

3. I _____ french fries.

4. My partner _____ french fries.

5. I _____ pizza.

I like pizza.
I <u>don't</u> like pizza.

He like<u>s</u> pizza.
She like<u>s</u> pizza.
He <u>doesn't</u> like pizza.
She <u>doesn't</u> like pizza.

6. My partner _____ pizza.

7. I _____ ice cream.

8. My partner _____ ice cream.

C. Sit in a group. Talk and complete.

MY COMMUNITY

A good Chinese restaurant in my area is _____.

A good Mexican restaurant in my area is _____.

A good Italian restaurant in my area is _____.

A good _____ restaurant in my area is _____.

A good fast-food restaurant in my area is _____.

A good pizzeria in my area is _____.

Using Your English: Ordering Lunch

 A. Listen.

1.

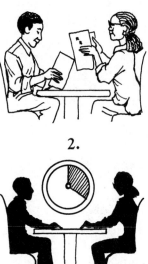

2.

3.

4.

5.

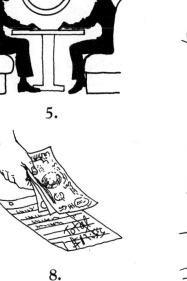

6.

7.

8.

9.

 B. Listen and find the picture.

C. Listen and repeat.

D. Practice with a partner.

E. Act it out.

> *Culture Note*
> Americans leave a tip for
> the waiter or the waitress.
> Excellent service–20%
> Good service–15%
> Fair service–10%

A. Read.

I live with my parents. My mother is home all day, so she cooks dinner. In the afternoon, she walks to the supermarket and buys food. We are from Italy, so she buys cheese, bread, meat, and fresh vegetables. She cooks all afternoon. When I come home, the house smells wonderful. I go into the kitchen and talk to my mother, and sometimes I help her. She always cooks pasta. Sometimes she makes her own pasta. She always makes a fresh salad. At dinnertime, everything is delicious! My mother is a wonderful cook.

B. Write about meals at your home. Your teacher will help you with your story.

_____

_____

_____

_____

_____

_____

_____

_____

The Big Picture: At the Restaurant

A. Listen.

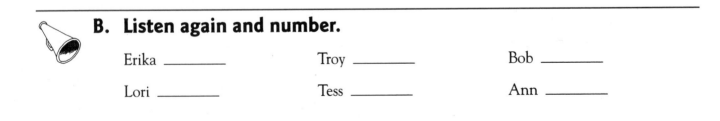

B. Listen again and number.

Erika _____   Troy _____   Bob _____

Lori _____   Tess _____   Ann _____

C. Listen and circle.

1. Yes (No)   5. Yes No

2. Yes No   6. Yes No

3. Yes No   7. Yes No

4. Yes No   8. Yes No

D. Listen and circle.

1. **a.** At night   (**b.**) Friday   **c.** At a table

2. **a.** Near the door   **b.** Near the window   **c.** They're eating

3. **a.** The menu   **b.** Dinner   **c.** The waitress

4. **a.** Chicken   **b.** Pizza   **c.** The menu

5. **a.** At a table   **b.** Pizza   **c.** Soda

6. **a.** Coffee   **b.** Soda   **c.** Yes, they are.

E. Complete.

1. Troy and Erika _____*are eating*_____ at Mario's.

2. Erika _____ at the menu.

3. Troy _____ spaghetti.

4. The waitress _____ their order.

5. The family _____ a big pizza.

6. They _____ soda.

> is ordering
>
> is eating
>
> ✓ are eating
>
> are drinking
>
> is taking
>
> is looking

F. Write.

Write about the picture.

Write a conversation between two people in the restaurant.

A. Complete.

1. I like _____ for breakfast.

2. I sometimes eat _____ for breakfast.

3. I always drink _____ for breakfast.

4. I like _____ or _____ for lunch.

5. I don't like _____ for lunch.

6. I never eat _____ for lunch.

7. I like _____ or _____ for dinner.

8. I never eat _____ for dinner.

9. I sometimes drink _____ for dinner.

10. I like _____ for dessert.

B. Put this conversation in order. Then write it.

_____ I'll have a turkey sandwich on a roll.

_____ Yes. Lettuce and tomato.

_____ Anything to drink?

___1___ Are you ready to order?

_____ Coffee, please.

_____ Lettuce and tomato?

Waitress: _Are you ready to order?_____

Customer: _____

Waitress: _____

Customer: _____

Waitress: _____

Customer: _____

A. What is the total? How much tip will you leave?

Hill's Diner

Scrambled eggs	$3.00
Juice	.75
Coffee	.75
Total	

Mario's Italian Restaurant

2 salads	$8.00
Spaghetti	9.50
Chicken	12.50
2 coffees	2.50
Total	

B. Put prices. What's the total? How much tip will you leave?

Sam's Cafe

Tuna Sandwich	_____
Vegetable soup	_____
Iced tea	_____
Total	

Summary

1. Present tense

I **like** chicken.

I **don't like** chicken.

He **likes** bananas.

He **doesn't like** bananas.

2. Adverbs of frequency

I **always** drink juice.　　She **always** eats a big breakfast.

I **sometimes** drink soda.　　She **sometimes** eats lunch.

I **never** drink coffee.　　She **never** eats a big dinner.

Dictionary

A. Listen and repeat.

Adjectives

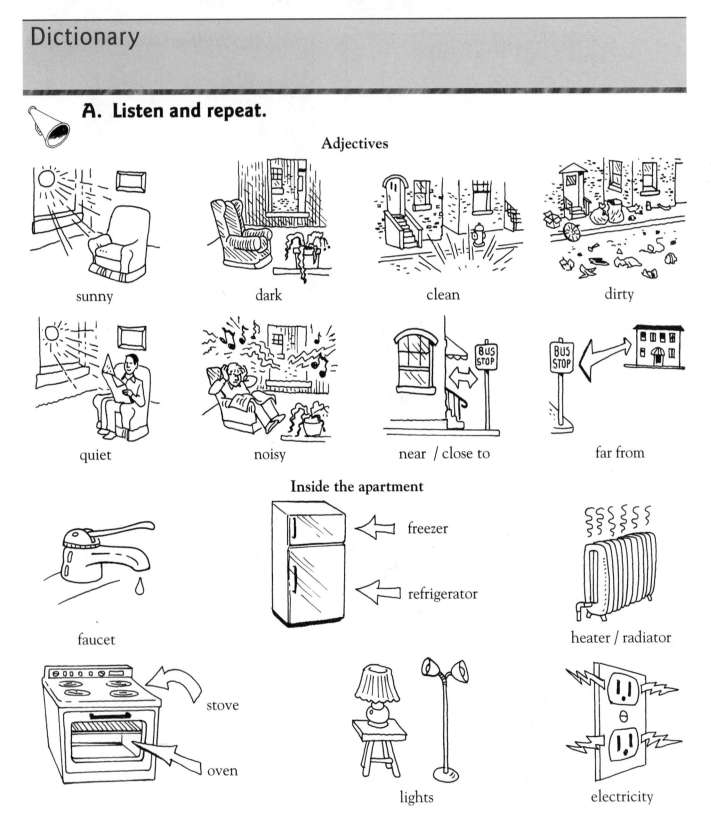

sunny

dark

clean

dirty

quiet

noisy

near / close to

far from

Inside the apartment

faucet

freezer

refrigerator

heater / radiator

stove

oven

lights

electricity

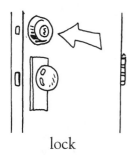

lock

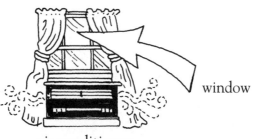

window

ceiling

Problems in the apartment

air conditioner

The faucet is leaking.

The paint is peeling.

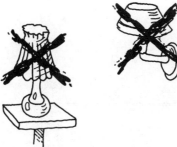

The air conditioner isn't working.

The stove isn't working.

The lights aren't working.

The freezer is broken.

The lock is broken.

The heat is off.

The electricity is off.

The window is stuck.

There's a mouse.

There are cockroaches.

133

Grammar in Action

A. Listen and circle.

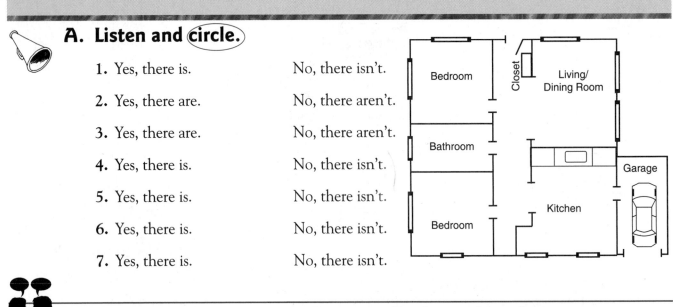

1. Yes, there is.   No, there isn't.
2. Yes, there are.   No, there aren't.
3. Yes, there are.   No, there aren't.
4. Yes, there is.   No, there isn't.
5. Yes, there is.   No, there isn't.
6. Yes, there is.   No, there isn't.
7. Yes, there is.   No, there isn't.

B. Sit in a group of four students. Talk about the apartment.

> **There is/There are**
> There is a large kitchen.
> There are two bedrooms.

C. Listen and write.

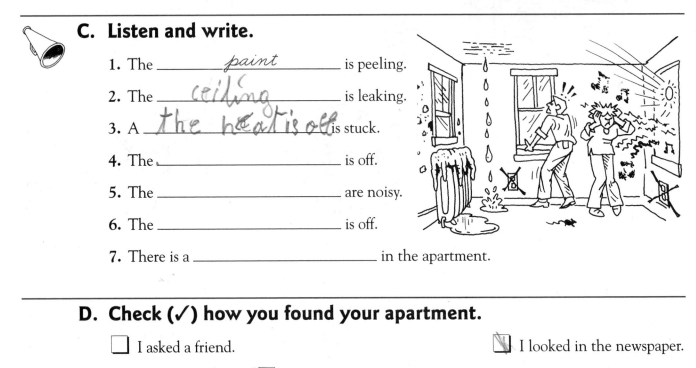

1. The _____paint_____ is peeling.
2. The _____ceiling_____ is leaking.
3. A __the heat is off__ is stuck.
4. The _____ is off.
5. The _____ are noisy.
6. The _____ is off.
7. There is a _____ in the apartment.

D. Check (✓) how you found your apartment.

☐ I asked a friend.   ☑ I looked in the newspaper.

☑ I saw a sign on a building.

What's the best way to find an apartment?

Reading the Classified Ads

A. Listen and repeat.

air conditioner	elevator	parking
apartment	furnished	pets
basement	included	security deposit
bath	large	transportation
bathroom	location	utilities
bedroom	modern	washer/dryer
carpeting		

Pets

B. Read and complete with a partner.

What does apt. mean?

apt.
a/c
BR
bsmt.
lge.
loc.
mod.
elev.
incl.
sec. dep.
utils.
w/d

1. Apt. means _____ *apartment* _____.
2. A/C means _____ large _____.
3. BR means _____ _____.
4. Bsmt. means _____ _____.
5. Lge. means _____ _____.
6. Mod. means _____ _____.
7. Elev. means _____ _____.
8. Incl. means _____ included _____.
9. Sec. dep. means _____ security deposit _____.
10. Utils. means _____ _____.
11. W/D means _____ _____.

C. Read and write.

For Rent
Lge. 1BR, w/ nice kitchen, sunny, elev. building w/ new windows, quiet, new carpet, no pets, uts. includ., near trans., sec. dep., $625/mo

1. It's _____ large _____.
2. It's _____ _____.
3. There is _____ _____.
4. It has _____ _____.
5. There is a _____ _____.
6. The rent is _____ _____.

D. Read and circle.

2 BR sunny apt., lge, new carpeting, utils. incl, 1-1/2 bath, no pets. sec. dep. $940	1. Yes **(No)**	The apartment has 3 bedrooms.
	2. Yes No	Utilities are included.
	3. Yes **No**	You can have a pet in the building.

3 lge. rooms, heat, hot water incl.Excellent loc., parking $650

1. Yes No   The rooms are large.

2. Yes No   Electricity is included.

3. Yes No   The apartment is in a good location.

3 BR house. 2-1/2 baths, no pets, a/c, utils incl,w/d, near beach $1900

1. Yes No   The house has 2-1/2 baths.

2. Yes No   There is a washer/dryer in the house.

3. Yes No   The house is near downtown.

Family house, 3 BR, 2 baths, liv. rm., hot water incl,parking, small pets ok, near transportation $1700

1. Yes No   The house has a dining room.

2. Yes No   All utilities are included.

3. Yes No   All pets are OK in this house.

E. Write a classified ad for your house or apartment.

F. Match.

1. How many bedrooms are there?

2. Where is the apartment?

3. Can I have a dog?

4. Is it near transportation?

5. Is there a laundry in the building?

6. How much is the rent?

7. Are utilities included?

8. Is there a parking lot?

• Yes, heat, electricity, and hot water are included.

• No. No pets are allowed.

• It's $540 a month.

• There are 2 bedrooms.

• No, but you can park on the street.

• Yes, the bus stop is on the corner, and the train station is three blocks away.

• No, but a Laundromat is on the corner.

• It's on Hope Street, across from the bank.

Calling the Super

A. Listen. Match the conversation and the problem. Then (circle) the time.

When will super be there?

a.	_6_	The lock is broken.	Right away	Later today	Tomorrow
b.	_3_	The faucet is leaking.	Right away	Later today	Tomorrow
c.	____	The stove isn't working.	Right away	Later today	Tomorrow
d.	_1_	The air conditioner isn't working.	(Right away)	Later today	Tomorrow
e.	_4_	There's a mouse in the kitchen.	Right away	Later today	Tomorrow
f.	_5_	There's a leak in the ceiling.	Right away	Later today	Tomorrow

B. Pair practice.

What's the problem?

The sink is leaking.

137

My Community

A. Read and complete.

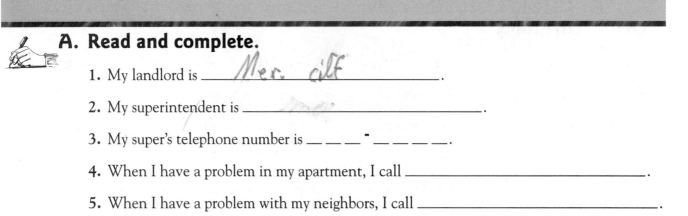

1. My landlord is _____ Mer. olf _____.

2. My superintendent is _____.

3. My super's telephone number is __ __ __ - __ __ __ __.

4. When I have a problem in my apartment, I call _____.

5. When I have a problem with my neighbors, I call _____.

B. Read and complete with *must* or *must not*.

Apartment Rules
Pay rent on time.
Be quiet.
Lock your doors.
No pets.
No smoking in the hallways.
Put cans and bottles in recycle bins.

1. Elaine and Peter _____ *must* _____ pay the rent on time.

2. Elaine and Peter _____ be quiet.

3. They _____ have a cat or a dog.

4. They _____ lock their doors.

5. They _____ smoke in the hallways.

6. They _____ put cans and bottles in the recycle bins.

> *Must/Must not*
> I **must pay** my rent on time.
> I **must not pay** my rent late.

> *Culture Note*
> In the U.S., many states require residents to *recycle* their empty cans and bottles.

C. Write four rules about your apartment or house.

1. I must _____

2. I must _____

3. I must not _____

4. I must not _____ hõ cHILder _____

D. Read your rules to a partner.

Working Together: Your Apartment

A. Check (✓) the true sentences about your apartment or house.

☒ 1. My apartment is sunny.

☒ 2. My apartment has two bedrooms.

☐ 3. My apartment has a large kitchen.

☐ 4. My apartment is near transportation.

☐ 5. My apartment is noisy.

☐ 6. My apartment is close to school.

☐ 7. My apartment is in a safe neighborhood.

☐ 8. There is an elevator in my building.

☐ 9. There is a laundry room in my building.

B. Interview two students about their apartments.

Questions	Partner 1: _____		Partner 2: _____	
1. Is your apartment sunny?	Yes	No	Yes	No
2. Are there two bedrooms in your apartment?	Yes	No	Yes	No
3. Is your kitchen large?	Yes	No	Yes	No
4. Is your apartment near transportation?	Yes	No	Yes	No
5. Is your apartment noisy?	Yes	No	Yes	No
6. Is your apartment close to school?	Yes	No	Yes	No
7. Is the neighborhood safe?	Yes	No	Yes	No
8. Is there an elevator in your building?	Yes	No	Yes	No
9. Is there a laundry room in your building?	Yes	No	Yes	No

C. Read and practice.

A: Hello, I'm calling about the one-bedroom apartment.

B: Well, it's a nice apartment, and it's sunny.

A: Does the rent include utilities?

B: It includes heat and hot water.

A: Is it near transportation?

B: Yes, it's near the bus stop.

A: Is there an elevator in the building?

B: No, there isn't.

A: When can I see the apartment?

B: You can see it tomorrow morning.

> *Culture Note*
> In the U.S., people often have to make an appointment to look at an apartment.

D. Complete with a partner.

A: Hello, I'm calling about the ___ol___- bedroom apartment.

B: Well, it's a _____ apartment, and it's _____.

A: Does the rent include utilities?

B: It includes _____.

A: Is it near _____?

B: _____.

A: Is there _____ in the building?

B: _____.

A: When can I see the apartment?

B: You can see it _____.

E. Act out your conversation.

A. Read.

I live in a two-bedroom apartment with my (wife) and three children. We are looking for a new apartment because this apartment is too small. Also, this apartment has many problems. The air conditioner isn't working, the paint is peeling, and the sink is leaking. We want to live in a better neighborhood. Our neighborhood isn't safe at night, and the streets are very dirty.

We want a sunny apartment with three bedrooms. We want a washer in our apartment if possible. We want to live near stores and transportation. We want an apartment that is close to everything we need.

B. Write about your house or apartment and neighborhood.

I live in a(n) _____. I like/don't like my _____.

It's _____ and _____

_____

_____

_____

_____

_____

The Big Picture: My Neighborhood

A. Listen.

B. Listen and circle.

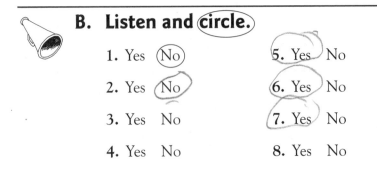

1. Yes (No)
2. Yes (No)
3. Yes No
4. Yes No
5. Yes No
6. Yes No
7. Yes No
8. Yes No

C. Listen and complete.

1. There is _____ *one* __Kitchen__ *bedroom* _____ in the apartment.

2. There is a _____ _____ in the apartment.

3. There are ___Bus Stop___ _____ in the apartment.

4. There isn't an _____ in the building.

5. There aren't any _____ in the building.

6. There's a _____ down the street.

7. There is a _____ _____ near the building.

8. The _____ are _____ and _____ .

D. Complete.

| across from |
| between |
| next to |

1. The Laundromat is _____ *next to* _____ Anna's building.

2. The park is _____ Anna's building.

3. The bus stop is _____ Anna's building.

4. The bus stop is _____ the post office and the library.

5. The market is _____ the school.

6. The parking lot is _____ Anna's building.

7. The bank is _____ the telephone company.

8. The Laundromat is _____ Anna's building and the market.

E. Pair practice. Where does she . . . ?

buy fruit

cash her check

get books

pay the telephone bill

wash her clothes

work

Where does she work?

She works at the school.

school

Laundromat

bookstore

bank

telephone company

supermarket

Practicing on Your Own

A. Read and complete.

1. The lock is _____ *broken* _____ .

2. There is a _____ *amus* _____ in the hallway.

3. The air _____ _____ _____ .

4. The paint _*Pelr*_ _____ .

5. The apartment is _____ .

6. There _____ two _____ in the apartment.

7. The apartment isn't _*pi diez*_ .

B. Look at the map of a neighborhood. Complete each question and answer.

1. _*Is*_ _*there*_ a bus stop near the apartment?   Yes, there _*is*_ .

2. _*IS*_ there a bank _____ the neighborhood?   No, there _____ .

3. Is the bakery _*Nex to*_ _____ the library?   No, it _____ .

4. Is _*ther is*_ a bookstore in the neighborhood?   Yes, _*I*_ _____ .

5. Is the apartment building _*acros from*_ the Laundromat?   Yes, _*I*_ _*S*_ .

6. _____ there any parking lots in the neighborhood?   Yes, _____ are.

144

A. Complete.

Lease

_____ _____ _____
Last Name   First Name   MI

        Rojas   *Maria*

_____ _____ _____
Spouse's Last Name   First Name   MI

Number of Occupants _____*
*No more than 5 occupants in one apartment

_____ _____ _____
Place of Employment   City   State

_____ Year of Employment   Occupation _____

References

_____ (   ) _____
Name of Reference (Not a relative)   Tel.

_____
Name of Bank   Address   Account Number

_____ _____ _____ _____
Signature of tenant   Date   Signature of spouse   Date

Summary

1. Present continuous

The faucet **is leaking.**

The air conditioner **isn't working.**

The lights **aren't working.**

2. *There is/There are*

There is a large kitchen.	**Is there** a large kitchen?	Yes, there is.
There are two bedrooms.	**Are there** three bedrooms?	No, there aren't.

3. Adjectives

The freezer is **broken**.   The window is **stuck**.

4. Must/Must not

I **must pay** the rent on time.

I **must not pay** the rent late.

11 Applying for a Job

Dictionary

A. Listen and repeat.

Hotel occupations

bellhop

desk clerk

valet

piano player   singer

bartender

cook

148

waiter   waitress   landscaper   maintenance mechanic

housekeeper   laundry worker   manager

Grammar in Action
Hotel Staff

A. Match.

c	1. A landscaper	a.	repairs equipment
e	2. A bellhop	b.	parks cars
a	3. A maintenance mechanic	c.	cuts the grass
b	4. A valet	d.	makes drinks
d	5. A bartender	e.	carries bags
i	6. A waitress	f.	washes sheets and towels
h	7. A desk clerk	g.	sings songs
f	8. A laundry worker	h.	registers guests
j	9. A housekeeper	i.	takes food orders
g	10. A singer	j.	cleans hotel rooms

B. Complete with a partner.

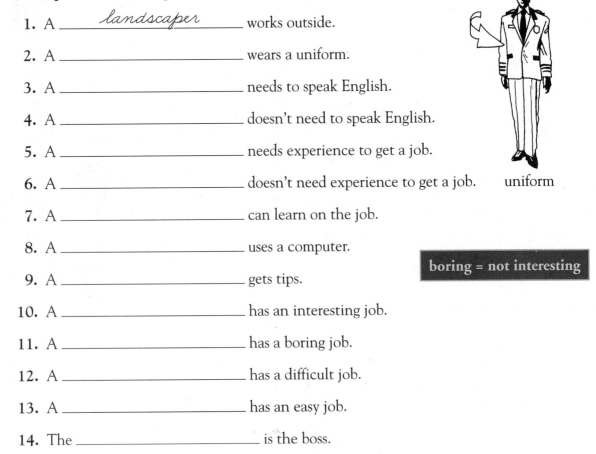

1. A _____*landscaper*_____ works outside.

2. A _____ wears a uniform.

3. A _____ needs to speak English.

4. A _____ doesn't need to speak English.

5. A _____ needs experience to get a job.

6. A _____ doesn't need experience to get a job.

7. A _____ can learn on the job.

8. A _____ uses a computer.

9. A _____ gets tips.

10. A _____ has an interesting job.

11. A _____ has a boring job.

12. A _____ has a difficult job.

13. A _____ has an easy job.

14. The _____ is the boss.

uniform

boring = not interesting

150

Job Skills and Experience

A. Listen to each person talk about his or her job experience. Write the number of the speaker under each picture.

_____   ___/___   _____   _____

B. Check (✓) your job skills.

- [✓] 1. I can speak a little English.
- [✓] 2. I can speak English well.
- [✓] 3. I can clean a room.
- [ ] 4. I can repair equipment.
- [ ] 5. I can play the piano.
- [ ] 6. I can sing well.
- [ ] 7. I can operate a riding lawn mower.
- [ ] 8. I can make drinks.
- [ ] 9. I can cook well.
- [ ] 10. I can drive a car.
- [ ] 11. I can carry heavy bags.
- [ ] 12. I can use a computer.
- [ ] 13. I can _____.

riding lawn mower

C. Read your job skills to a partner.

D. Complete.

In my country, I was a _____ sewer _____.

In my last job, I was a _____.

Now I am a _____.

I can _____.

I can _____.

I can _____.

Job Experience

A. Listen and read.

Work Experience			
From	To	Employer	Position
1996	2000	The Flamingo	cook
1992	1996	Tio Pepe	waiter

Alex: I'm applying for a job as a cook.

Manager: Do you have any experience?

Alex: Yes, I was a cook at The Flamingo in Tampa.

Manager: When?

Alex: From 1996 to 2000. And I was a waiter at Tio Pepe in Cancún from 1992 to 1996.

B. Pair practice.

Do you have any experience?

Yes, I was a desk clerk at Ocean Resort.

When?

From 1997 to 1999.

1. B&B Lawn Care
   1995–1999

2. The Copa
   1998–2000

3. The Manor Hotel
   _____ – _____

4. City Hospital
   _____ – _____

C. Complete with your work experience.

Work Experience			
From	To	Employer	Position
2001	2000		

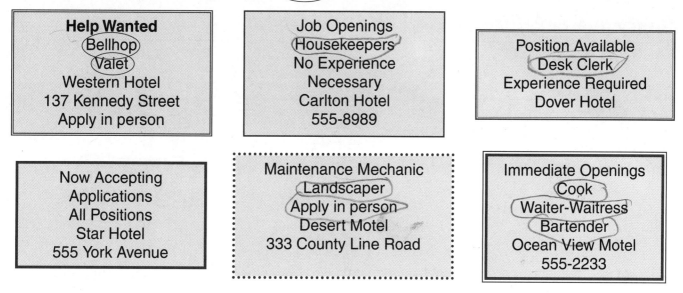

D. Tell a partner about your work experience.

Job Ads

A. Read these job ads. Circle the jobs.

Help Wanted
Bellhop
Valet
Western Hotel
137 Kennedy Street
Apply in person

Job Openings
Housekeepers
No Experience
Necessary
Carlton Hotel
555-8989

Position Available
Desk Clerk
Experience Required
Dover Hotel

Now Accepting
Applications
All Positions
Star Hotel
555 York Avenue

Maintenance Mechanic
Landscaper
Apply in person
Desert Motel
333 County Line Road

Immediate Openings
Cook
Waiter-Waitress
Bartender
Ocean View Motel
555-2233

B. Read these classified ads from a newspaper. Check (✓) the information below.

COOK FT 2 years experience required. Excellent pay w/benefits. Call Thurs. – Sat 11:00AM – 4:00 PM. 555-2126

A

FRONT DESK CLERK for Hotel PT Shift 3PM – 11PM Will train. Apply in person. Plaza Hotel. Seaside.

B

LANDSCAPER Immediate FT opening for landscape crew. Valid license required. $9.00/hour. Benefits, vacation. Call today 555-9328.

C

MAINTENANCE MECHANIC FT Must have painting, plumbing, & electrical skills. Salary based on experience. Great benefits. Sunrise Resort. 555-4343.

D

	A	B	C	D
1. This job is full time.	✓	☐	✓	✓
2. This job pays $9.00 an hour.	☐	☐	☐	☐
3. This job has benefits.	✓	✓	☐	☐
4. This job requires a driver's license.	☐	☐	☐	☐
5. This job requires experience.	☐	☐	☐	☐
6. This job is from 3:00 PM to 11:00 PM.	☐	☐	☐	☐
7. You can apply in person for this job.	☐	☐	☐	☐
8. You need to call about this job.	☐	☐	☐	☐
9. I would like this job.	☐	☐	☐	☐

Salary and Benefits

A. Read.

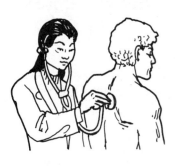

1. I have medical benefits.

2. I have a dental plan.

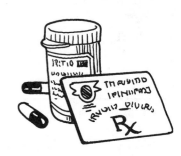

3. I have a prescription plan.

4. I have five sick days. **5.** I have two weeks' vacation. **6.** I have a retirement plan.

B. Complete about your benefits.

1. I **have / don't have** medical benefits.

2. I **have / don't have** a dental plan.

3. I **have / don't have** a prescription plan.

4. I have _cero_ sick days.

5. I have _____ weeks' vacation.

6. I also have _Prescriplioo_ .

 **C. Read your sentences to a partner.**

D. Listen and write the salary and benefits.

> *Culture Note*
> Usually the interviewer will tell you the salary and benefits during the interview. If not, it is OK to ask.

Employee	Salary	Overtime	Medical benefits	Dental plan	Rx plan	Sick days	Vacation
Karina	$8	$10	After 6 months			3	1 week
Mohamed	46						
Li-Ping	15,9	15 14					
Juan	15 14						

155

Application

A. Read and complete.

> Job Openings
> Housekeepers
> No Experience Necessary
> Carlton Hotel

CARLTON HOTEL

Position _____ housekeeper _____

Name _____ Marczak _____ Marta _____ E. _____
                   Last   First   Middle

Address __ 537 _____ Ocean Drive _____ Clearwater _____ FL __
              Number   Street   City   State

Social Security No. __ 123-45-6789 __   Date of birth __ 1 __/ 17 __/ 79 __

Telephone _____ 555-9424 _____   Marital status ☐ Married ☑ Single ☐ Divorced

Work Experience

From	To	Employer	Position
1996	200_	King Cruise Line	housekeeper

Signature of applicant _____ *Marta Marczak* _____

---

1. Marta is applying for a job as a _____ *housekeeper* _____.

2. She is applying for a job at _____.

3. Marta is _____ years old.

4. Marta was a _____ on the King Cruise Line.

5. She worked from _____ to _____.

B. Complete with your work experience.

CARLTON HOTEL

Position _____

Name _____

             Last   First   Middle

Address _____

     Number   Street   City   State

Social Security No. _____ Date of birth _____/_____/_____

Telephone _____ Marital status ☐ Married ☐ Single ☐ Divorced

Work Experience

From	To	Employer	Position

Signature of applicant _____

Interview

A. Read.

CARLTON HOTEL

Position _____ valet _____

Name _____ Moreno _____ Luis _____ A. _____
               Last   First   Middle

Address _____ 397 _____ Marina Way _____ Largo _____ FL _____
        Number   Street   City   State

Social Security No. _____ 987-65-4321 _____ Date of birth _6_ / _15_ / _80_

Telephone _____ 555-5321 _____ Marital status ☐ Married ☑ Single ☐ Divorced

Work Experience

From	To	Employer	Position
1999	200_	Cosimo's Pizza	delivery person

Signature of applicant _____ *Luis Moreno* _____

B. Listen and check (✓) *Yes* or *No*.

		Yes	No
1.	Luis is interviewing for a job as a valet.	☑	☐
2.	He has experience as a valet.	☐	☐
3.	Luis has a clean driver's license.	☐	☐
4.	Luis had an accident last year.	☐	☐
5.	Luis can drive a stick shift.	☐	☐
6.	Luis can start tomorrow.	☐	☐

7. This job is full time. ☐ ☐

8. The salary is $8.00 an hour. ☐ ☐

9. Luis will get tips. ☐ ☐

10. Luis can wear sneakers. ☐ ☐

C. Answer.

1. How many hours a week will Luis work? _____

2. How much will he make an hour? _____

3. How much will Luis make a week? _____

4. Will he receive tips? _____

Working Together

A. Read and practice.

A: I'm applying for a job as a bellhop.

B: Do you have any experience?

A: Yes. I was a valet at the Davis Hotel.

B: When?

A: From 1997 to 2000.

B: We have an opening on the second shift, from 3:00 PM to 11:00 PM.

A: What is the salary?

B: The salary is $6.00 an hour plus tips.

A: Are there benefits?

B: After six months, you get medical benefits. And you have three sick days. The first year, you have one week vacation.

A: Good.

B: When can you start?

A: I can start tomorrow.

B: Okay. The first two days, Ricky will train you.

> *Culture Note*
> **Arrive five to ten minutes early for an interview.**

> *Culture Note*
> **Many jobs have two or three shifts, for example:**
> **First shift: 7:00 AM to 3:00 PM**
> **Second shift: 3:00 PM to 11:00 PM**
> **Third shift: 11:00 PM to 7:00 AM**

B. Complete with a partner. One student is the manager. One student is applying for a job.

A: I'm applying for a job as a _____.

B: Do you have any experience?

A: Yes. I was a _____ at _____.

B: When?

A: From _____ to _____.

B: We have an opening on the _____ shift, from _____ to _____.

A: What is the salary?

B: The salary is _____.

A: Are there benefits?

B: _____

_____

A: Good.

B: When can you start?

A: I can start _____.

B: OK. _____ will train you.

C. Act out your conversation.

D. Do you like your job? Check (✓) the things that people like about their jobs.

My boss is helpful. ✓   My coworkers are friendly.   I don't like my hours.

My salary is low.   I don't have any benefits.   The job is interesting.

The job is boring.   I have good benefits.   I get tips.

I stand all day.   I work very hard.

160

E. Interview two students about their jobs.

Questions	Student 1: _____		Student 2: _____	
1. Do you like your job?	Yes	No	Yes	No
2. Do you have an interesting job?	Yes	No	Yes	No
3. Do you like your hours?	Yes	No	Yes	No
4. Do you like your boss?	Yes	No	Yes	No
5. Do you stand at work?	Yes	No	Yes	No
6. Do you use a computer at work?	Yes	No	Yes	No
7. Do you speak English at work?	Yes	No	Yes	No
8. Do you get tips?	Yes	No	Yes	No
9. Do you like your coworkers?	Yes	No	Yes	No
10. Do you get benefits?	Yes	No	Yes	No

F. Check (✓) and discuss: How did you find your job?

☐ A friend told me about the job.

☐ My brother works there.

☐ I saw a Help Wanted sign.

☐ I looked in the classified ads in the newspaper.

☐ I stopped at a factory and spoke with the manager.

☐ I looked on the Internet.

☐ _____.

The Big Picture: The Sunrise Hotel

 A. Listen and circle.

1.	Ricardo is the day manager of the Sunrise Hotel.	Yes	(No)
2.	The hotel has more than 200 rooms.	Yes	No
3.	The hotel has about 200 employees.	Yes	No
4.	A courtesy van driver parks the guests' cars.	Yes	No
5.	The hotel has three shifts.	Yes	No
6.	Everyone works full time.	Yes	No
7.	People who work at night make a dollar extra an hour.	Yes	No
8.	The salary is high.	Yes	No
9.	Many employees get tips.	Yes	No
10.	This hotel has several openings.	Yes	No

B. Listen. Who is the manager speaking to?

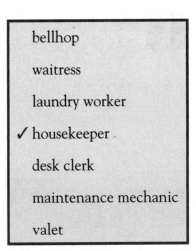

1. He's speaking to the ___*housekeeper*___.

2. He's speaking to the _____.

3. He's speaking to the _____.

4. He's speaking to the _____.

5. He's speaking to the _____.

6. He's speaking to the _____.

7. He's speaking to the _____.

| bellhop |
| waitress |
| laundry worker |
| ✓ housekeeper |
| desk clerk |
| maintenance mechanic |
| valet |

C. Complete.

| is | earns | works | likes | gets |

1. Shelley ___*works*___ at the Sunrise Hotel. She _____ a desk clerk. She _____ from 11:00 to 7:00. She _____ the hours because she can be home with her children in the daytime. She _____ $10.00 an hour.

2. Chin-Kun _____ at the Sunrise Hotel. He _____ a bartender. He _____ from 4:00 to 1:00 on Friday, Saturday, and Sunday. Chin-Kun _____ a teacher during the week. He _____ extra money at the hotel.

3. Kasia _____ a waitress at the Sunrise Hotel. She _____ from 7:00 AM to 3:00 PM. She _____ her job. Kasia _____ $6.00 an hour. She _____ very friendly, so she _____ good tips.

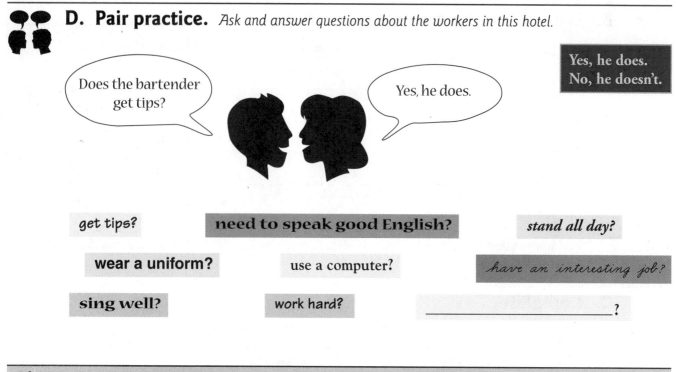

Does the bartender get tips?

Yes, he does.

Yes, he does.
No, he doesn't.

get tips?   need to speak good English?   *stand all day?*

wear a uniform?   use a computer?   *have an interesting job?*

sing well?   work hard?   _____?

Sharing Our Stories

A. Read.

> *I am a desk clerk at a small motel near a busy highway. The motel has about 50 rooms. Most guests are driving a long distance and need a room to stay for the night. I check people into and out of the motel. I use a computer to type the person's name and address. Most guests pay by credit card. I also take reservations on the telephone and give information and directions to the guests. I enjoy my job. The manager is helpful, and my hours are great. I work from 3:00 PM to 11:00 PM. I'm busy from 4:00 to 9:00, when most people check in. My salary is low, but the work isn't hard. From 9:00 to 11:00, it's very quiet. I can read or study.*

B. Complete these sentences about your job.

I like _____ .

I like _____ .

I don't like _____ .

I don't like _____ .

C. Write about your job.

1. Explain your job.

2. What do you like about your job?

3. What don't you like about your job?

Practicing on Your Own

A. Complete.

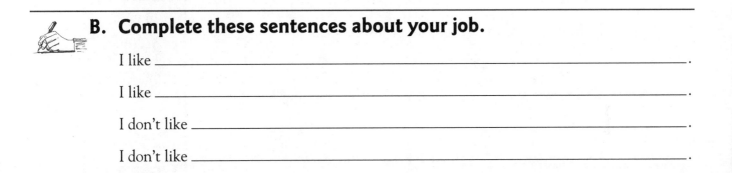

Michelle _*has*_ experience _*as*_ _*a*_ _*bartender*_ . She _*was*_ a _*bartender*_ from 1997 _*to*_ 2000.

Rima _____ experience _____ ____ _____ . She _____ a _____ 1996 ____ 1999.

Kathy _____ experience _____ ____ _____ . She _____ a _____ _____ _____ ____ ____ .

B. Answer.

1. Do you work at a hotel? _____

2. Do you work at night? _____

3. Do you wear a uniform? _____

4. Do you get tips? _____

5. Do you have medical benefits? _____

6. Do you like your boss? _____

C. Complete.

likes   doesn't like

| all night |
| friendly |
| low |
| ✓ interesting |
| boring |
| helpful |

1. Tony ____likes____ his job because it is

____interesting____ .

2. Henry _____ his coworkers because they are

_____ .

3. Julia _____ her job because she works

_____ .

4. Yuri _____ his job because his salary is _____ .

5. Steven _____ his job because it is _____ .

6. Monica _____ her boss because she is _____ .

7. I **like/don't like** my job because _____ .

Looking at Numbers

A. Figure it out!

1. Martin is a desk clerk. He makes $10.00 an hour. He works 40 hours a week. What is his weekly salary?

2. Tom is a maintenance mechanic. He works 40 hours a week and makes $15.00 an hour. How much does he earn a week?

3. Myra works part time as a housekeeper. She earns $8.00 an hour. She works 15 hours a week. What is her weekly salary?

4. Susan works 40 hours a week as a cook and makes $9.00 an hour. She works 10 hours overtime and makes $11.00 an hour. What is her weekly salary?

5. Tina is a bellhop. She works 10 hours a day. Tina makes $4.00 an hour. She usually makes $100.00 a day in tips. How much does she make a day?

Summary

1. Present tense

I **wear** a uniform.	I **don't wear** a uniform.
I **have** an interesting job.	I **don't have** an interesting job.
He **wears** a uniform.	He **doesn't wear** a uniform.
He **has** medical benefits.	He **doesn't have** medical benefits.

2. *Yes/No questions*

Do you **like** your job?	Yes, I **do.**	No, I **don't.**
Does she **like** her job?	Yes, she **does.**	No, she **doesn't.**

3. Past *be*

I **am** a cook at the Flamingo. (now)

I **was** a cook at the Flamingo. (past)

4. *Can*

I **can play** the piano.

He **can repair** equipment.

Can you **use** a computer?

Can she **speak** English?

12 Transportation

Dictionary

A. Listen and repeat.

Transportation

I walk.

I drive.

I ride my bike.

My friend gives me
a ride.

I take the bus.

I take the train.

I take the subway.

I take a taxi.

Weather

It's sunny.

It's cloudy.

It's windy.

It's raining.

It's snowing.

It's hot.

It's warm.

It's cool.

It's cold.

90° °F

75° °F

50° °F

20° °F

Grammar in Action
Where's the Park?

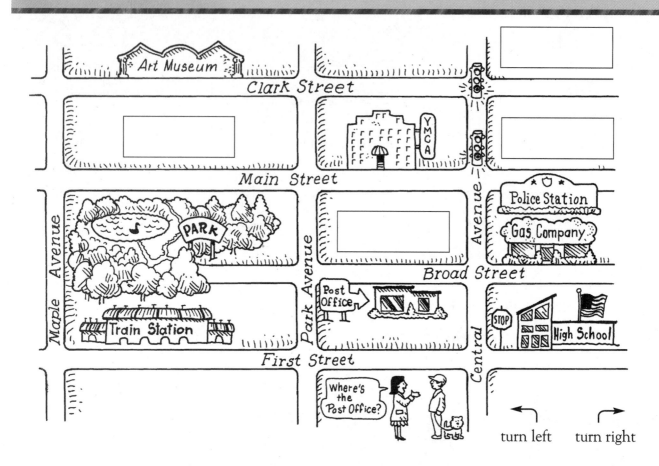

turn left   turn right

A. Read and follow these directions on the map.

1. **A:** Where's the post office?
   B: Walk two blocks to Broad Street.
   Turn left.
   The post office is on your left.

2. **A:** Where's the art museum?
   B: Walk four blocks to the second traffic light. That's Clark Street.
   Turn left.
   The art museum is about two blocks up on your right.

3. **A:** Where's the high school?
   B: Walk one block to the first stop sign. That's First Street.
   Turn right.
   The high school is on your left.

traffic light

stop sign

B. Listen and write the locations on the map.

1. City Hall   2. library   3. hospital   4. aquarium

C. Read and complete.

1. **A:** Where's the gas company?

   B: Walk two blocks to _____Broad_____ Street.

   Turn _____.

   The gas company is on your _____.

2. **A:** Where's the train station?

   B: Walk one block to the first _____.

   That's _____ Street.

   Turn _____.

   The train station is two blocks up on your _____.

3. **A:** Where's the park?

   B: Walk two blocks to _____ Street.

   Turn _____.

   The park is about two blocks up, in front of you.

traffic light
stop sign
right
left
Clark
Main
✓ Broad
First

D. With a partner, write the directions to each of these locations.

1. City Hall   2. police station   3. aquarium

Walk _____ blocks.
Walk _____ blocks to the first _____.
That's _____ Street.
Turn right. Turn left.
The _____ is on your right/left.

The Bus

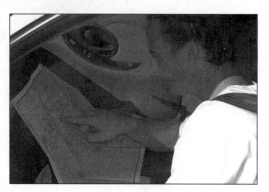

A: How do I get to the zoo?

B: Take the 21 Bus. Get off at State Street.

B. Listen and write the bus number. (Circle) the street name.

	Bus Number		Street	
	_14_		Georges Avenue	(Jackson Avenue)
a.	_____		Main Street	Maple Street
b.	_____		Park Avenue	Clark Avenue
c.	_____		First Street	Fourth Street
d.	_____		Broad Street	Bay Street
e.	_____		Central Avenue	Center Avenue

Bus Schedule

A. Read.

49 - Bus Schedule

Main	7:00 AM
	7:30 AM
7th	8:00 AM
	8:30 AM
23rd	9:00 AM
	Every hour
52nd	5:00 PM
	5:30 PM
	6:00 PM
	6:30 PM
Park	7:00 PM
	Every hour
Central	Until 10 PM

State   Bay   Mall

1. A: It's 7:10 AM. When's the next bus?

   B: At 7:30.

2. A: It's 5:15 PM. When's the next bus?

   B: At 5:30.

B. Pair practice. *Ask about the next bus.*

1. It's 8:45. A.M.

2. It's 11:05. A.M.

3. It's 2:00. P.M.

4. It's 6:10. P.M.

Weather

A. Listen to the weather. Find the city and write the temperature on the map.

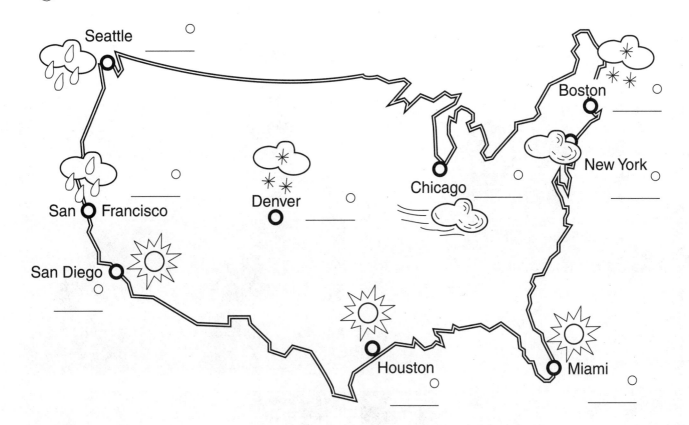

B. Write the weather conditions from the map above.

It's _____ *snowing and cold* _____ in Boston.

It's _____ in New York.

It's _____ in Miami.

It's _____ in Houston.

It's _____ in San Diego.

It's _____ in San Francisco.

It's _____ in Seattle.

It's _____ in Denver.

It's _____ in Chicago.

| cold |
| cloudy |
| raining |
| windy |
| snowing |
| hot |
| warm |
| cool |
| cold |

C. Sit in a group. Discuss these pictures.

What's the weather?

What is each person doing?

What is each person wearing?

D. Read.

1.

Future Tense
I <u>am going</u> to drive.
He <u>is going</u> to drive.
She <u>is going</u> to drive.
They <u>are going</u> to drive.

It's raining.
Bob is going to the art museum.
He is going to take the subway.

2.

It's a hot, sunny day.
Marie is going to the beach.
She is going to drive.

3.

It's snowing hard.
Nita isn't going out.
She is going to stay home.

E. Pair practice. *Answer with a partner.*

1. What's the weather?

2. Where is Diego going?

3. How is he going to get there?

4. What's the weather?

5. Where are Olga and Aron going?

6. How are they going to get there?

7. What's the weather? _____

8. Where are you going? _____

9. How are you going to get there? _____

Working Together
Using Your English: *The Bus Ride*

 A. Listen.

1.
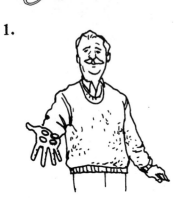

2.

3.
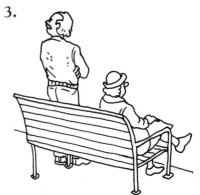

4.

5.

6.

7.

8.

9.

B. Listen and find the picture.

Culture Note
You must have exact change or a token to take the bus.

C. Listen and repeat.

D. Practice with a partner.

E. Act it out.

F. Interview three students.

How do you get to school?

I take the bus.

	Student 1 _____	**Student 2** _____	**Student 3** _____
Work			
School			
Supermarket			
Library			

G. Discuss with a group.

1. Is there a train station near your school?

2. Where is it?

3. Is there a bus stop near your school?

4. Where is it?

5. Is there a subway in your city?

6. Where is the nearest stop?

7. Do you take public transportation to school? What is the fare?

8. Where is the closest airport to your school?

177

The Weather Map

A. Complete.

Bring in the local newspaper. Look at the weather map. Circle the words you know. What is the weather today? What is the weather for tomorrow?

Today, it's _____ and

_____ .

The temperature is _____°.

In my country, the weather now is _____ .

cold
cool
warm
hot
cloudy
sunny
windy
raining
snowing

Sharing Our Stories

A. Read.

My wife and I live in a small city. We have one car. Sometimes transportation is a problem.

My wife is a manicurist. She works at a beauty salon about one mile from our house. She usually walks to work. When it's raining, a beautician at the same salon gives her a ride.

I am a cook at a large hotel. I work about fifteen miles from here. I drive to work every day.

We have two children, ages ten and twelve. They take the bus to school. The bus stop is on the corner near our house. When it is raining, they wear their raincoats and take their umbrellas.

B. Check (✓) and complete the sentences that are true for you.

☐ I have a car.

☐ I don't have a car.

☐ Transportation is a problem in my family.

☐ Transportation isn't a problem in my family.

☐ I work.

   I live _____ miles from work.

   I _____ to work.

☐ I go to school.

   I live _____ miles from school.

   I _____ to school.

☐ I give _____ a ride.

C. Write.

Use the information above to write about transportation and your family. Where do people have to go? How do they get there?

The Big Picture: Traffic

A. Listen.

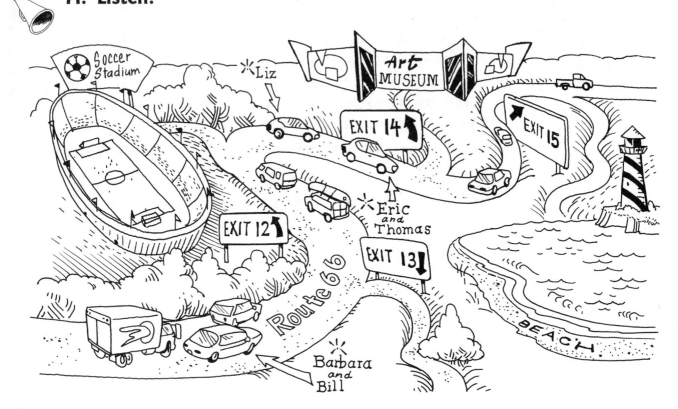

B. Listen and circle.

1. **a.** It's sunny and hot.   **b.** The traffic is heavy.   **c.** They're on the road.

2. **a.** at a soccer game   **b.** hot   **c.** in their car

3. **a.** to the beach   **b.** to a soccer game   **c.** on the highway

4. **a.** on the highway   **b.** at the museum   **c.** at Exit 14

5. **a.** visit a museum   **b.** fish   **c.** She's driving.

6. **a.** on the highway   **b.** at the beach   **c.** at Exit 12

7. **a.** to visit Liz   **b.** to the beach   **c.** to a soccer game

Culture Note
Do not give a ride to people on the road.

C. Listen and write the road number and the exit number.

              Road   Exit

1. Highway _____   _____

2. Route _____   _____

3. Interstate _____   _____

4. Freeway _____   _____

5. Route _____   _____

6. Highway _____   _____

D. Complete.

get	
fish	
get	
visit	
watch	

1. Barbara and Bill _are_ _going_ _to_ _get_ off at Exit 12.

2. They _____ _____ _____ _____ a soccer game.

3. Liz _____ _____ _____ _____ off at Exit 14.

4. She _____ _____ _____ _____ the art museum.

5. Eric and Thomas _____ _____ _____ _____ off at Exit 15.

6. They _____ _____ _____ _____ the beach.

7. They _____ _____ _____ _____ all day.

> **Future Tense**
> I **am going to drive.**
> He **is going to drive.**
> She **is going to drive.**
> They **are going to drive.**

E. Talk about the meaning of each sign or situation.

> **Must**
> You **must** stop.
> drive slowly.

> **Must not**
> You **must not** park here.
> turn right.

F. Draw a sign that you see in your neighborhood. What does it mean?

Practicing on Your Own

A. Answer.

> Yes, it is.
> No, it isn't.

Boston 20°

1. Is it raining in Boston? ___No, it isn't.___
2. Is it snowing in Boston? _____
3. Is it cold there? _____

HOUSTON 70°

4. Is it hot in Houston? _____
5. Is it sunny in Houston? _____
6. Is it going to rain there? _____

Seattle 50°

7. Is it cool in Seattle? _____
8. Is it cloudy in Seattle? _____
9. Is it going to rain there? _____

B. Complete.

> *Future Tense*
> I **am going to drive.**
> He **is going to drive.**
> She **is going to drive.**
> They **are going to drive.**

take
visit
give
walk
study

1. Yelena ___is___ ___going___ ___to___ ___visit___ her sister in the hospital.

2. She _____ _____ _____ _____ a taxi.

3. Marie _____ _____ _____ the library.

4. Carlos and Diego _____ _____ _____ _____ the bus to work.

5. My car is at the garage. My friend _____ _____ _____ _____ me a ride.

6. It's a beautiful day. Pierre _____ _____ _____ _____ to work.

7. It's snowing. I _____.

8. It's a hot, sunny day. I _____.

Looking at Forms: A Parking Ticket

A. Read and answer the questions.

PARKING COMPLAINT		SUMMONS Q23456

YOU ARE HEREBY SUMMONED TO APPEAR BEFORE THE COURT TO ANSWER THIS COMPLAINT CHARGING YOU WITH UNLAWFUL PARKING.   **COURT DATE:** 4/1

Make of Vehicle	Year	Body Type
Ford	1998	Sedan

Color	Lic. Plate No.	State
Blue	ABC 123	N.Y.

Date of Offense	Hour	Location
3/15	3:00 pm	Main Street

PARKING OFFENSES

OFFENSE	PENALTY	OFFENSE	PENALTY
☑ Overtime Meter No. __1659__	$10.00	☐ Double Parking	$35.00
☐ Permit Parking (no Permit)	$20.00	☐ Prohibited Area	$35.00

1. PLEA OF NOT GUILTY If you intend to plead not guilty, you must notify the court within one week.
2. PLEA OF GUILTY If you intend to plead guilty, complete the Appearance, Plea and Waiver section below. Bring or mail this summons and a check or money order to:

Plainville Town Violations Board
123 Main Street

APPEARANCE, PLEA AND WAIVER

By signing this document, I give up my right to a lawyer and I admit that I am guilty of the offense charged. I enclose payment of the noted penalty.

_____Tuan Nguyen_____   _____3/17_____
(Defendant's signature)   (Date)

Driver's License Number __1234 1234 1234 1234__ State: ____New York____

1. What kind of car does Tuan own?

2. What was his offense? What is the penalty?

3. When did he get his ticket?

4. Is Tuan guilty or not guilty?

5. Does he have to go to court?

Summary

1. Directions

Walk two blocks.

Turn right.

2. Present tense: *How* questions

How do you get to work?   I take the bus.

I drive.

3. Future tense

I **am going to walk** to the park.

He **is going to walk** to the park.

She **is going to walk** to the park.

You **are going to walk** to the park.

They **are going to walk** to the park.

4. *Must/Must not*

You **must stop.**

You **must not park** here.

13 A Visit to the Doctor

Dictionary

A. Listen and repeat.

Parts of the body

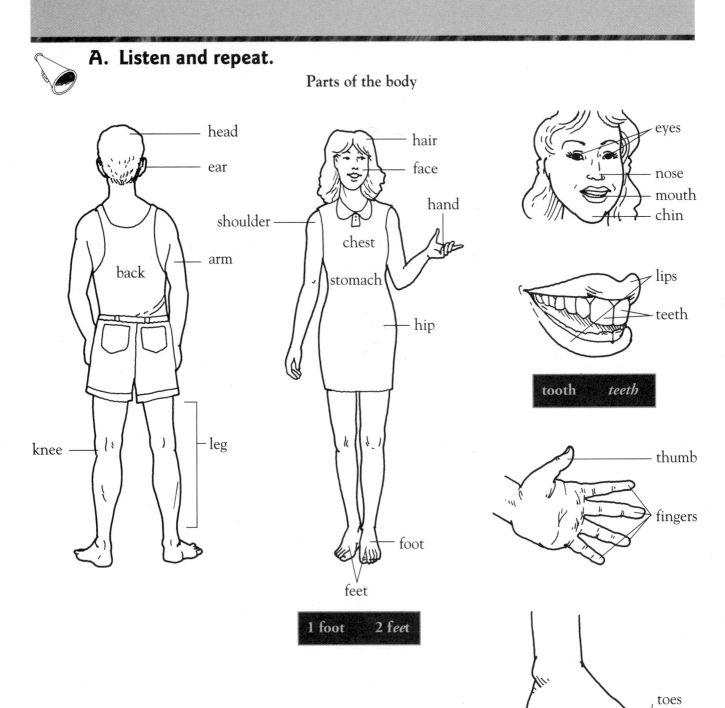

head
ear
shoulder
back
arm
knee
leg

hair
face
hand
chest
stomach
hip
foot
feet

1 foot   2 feet

eyes
nose
mouth
chin

lips
teeth

tooth   *teeth*

thumb
fingers

toes

Health problems

allergy

burn

cold

cough

fever

headache

sore throat

stomachache

toothache

Remedies

aspirin

ibuprofen

ice pack

heating pad

dentist

doctor

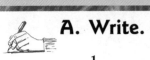 **A. Write.**

1.

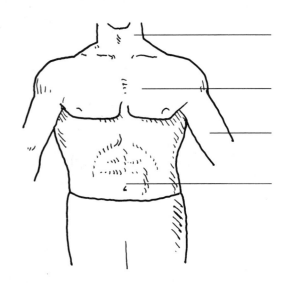

head	chin	eyes
ears	nose	lips

2.

arm	chest	stomach
	neck	

3.

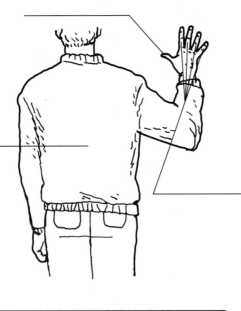

back	fingers	thumb

4.

foot	feet	knee	toe

Where does it hurt?

A. Listen and repeat.

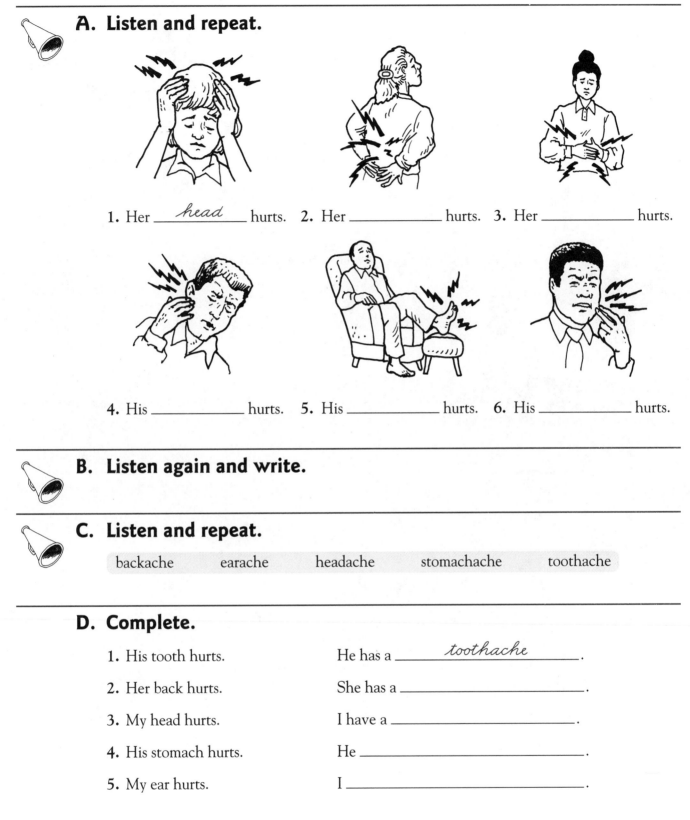

1. Her _____*head*_____ hurts. 2. Her _____ hurts. 3. Her _____ hurts.

4. His _____ hurts. 5. His _____ hurts. 6. His _____ hurts.

B. Listen again and write.

C. Listen and repeat.

backache   earache   headache   stomachache   toothache

D. Complete.

1. His tooth hurts.   He has a _____*toothache*_____.

2. Her back hurts.   She has a _____.

3. My head hurts.   I have a _____.

4. His stomach hurts.   He _____.

5. My ear hurts.   I _____.

Health Problems

A. Match.

	Have/Has	
He She	has	a sore throat.
They	have	allergies.

1.

2.

3.

4.

5.

6.

7.

8.

- She has a burn.

- She has a sore throat.

- They have allergies.

- They have colds.

- He has a headache.

- They have stomachaches.

- He has a cough.

- She has a fever.

190

Household Remedies

A. Listen and repeat.

1.

2.

3. IBUPROFEN

4.

5. ASPIRIN

6. JACKPO

7.

8. H₂O

B. Read and number.

_____ take aspirin   _____ drink liquids   _____ stay in bed

_____ call the doctor   _____ take ibuprofen   _____ use a heating pad

___1___ use an ice pack   _____ call the dentist

C. What are they going to do? Complete.

> I am going to ...
> He is going to ...
> She is going to ...
> They are going to ...

call the dentist	stay in bed
call the doctor	✓ take aspirin
drink soda	take ibuprofen
drink hot tea	take some medicine
	use a heating pad

1. She has a headache. She is going to ___*take aspirin*___.

2. He has a cough. He is going to _____.

3. They have sore throats. They are going to _____.

4. I have a backache. I am going to _____.

5. She has a toothache. She _____.

6. He has a stomachache. He _____.

7. They have bad colds. They _____.

8. I have a fever. I _____.

Reading Labels

A. Read the directions. Circle *must* or *must not*.

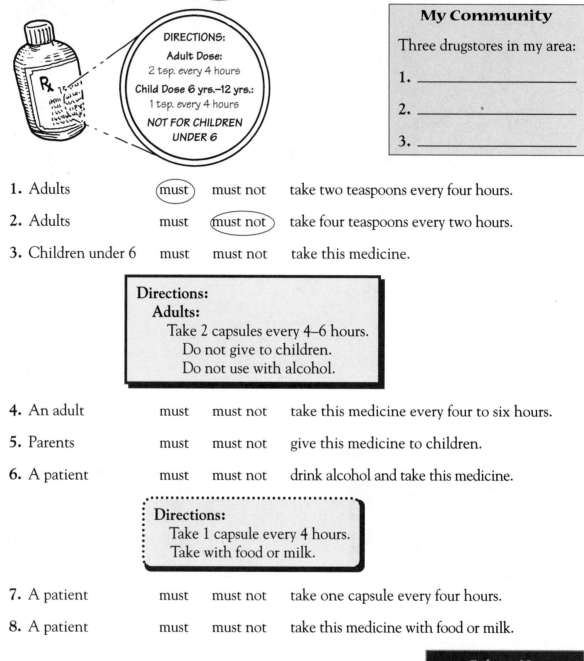

DIRECTIONS:

Adult Dose:
2 tsp. every 4 hours

Child Dose 6 yrs.–12 yrs.:
1 tsp. every 4 hours

NOT FOR CHILDREN
UNDER 6

My Community

Three drugstores in my area:

1. _____

2. _____

3. _____

1. Adults   (must)   must not   take two teaspoons every four hours.

2. Adults   must   (must not)   take four teaspoons every two hours.

3. Children under 6   must   must not   take this medicine.

Directions:
Adults:
    Take 2 capsules every 4–6 hours.
    Do not give to children.
    Do not use with alcohol.

4. An adult   must   must not   take this medicine every four to six hours.

5. Parents   must   must not   give this medicine to children.

6. A patient   must   must not   drink alcohol and take this medicine.

Directions:
    Take 1 capsule every 4 hours.
    Take with food or milk.

7. A patient   must   must not   take one capsule every four hours.

8. A patient   must   must not   take this medicine with food or milk.

Culture Note
To get a prescription,
you must see a doctor.

192

Working Together
Who's Your Doctor?

A. Complete.

My doctor is _____ .

My children's pediatrician is _____ .

My dentist is _____ .

My hospital is _____ .

My pharmacy is _____ .

> **Culture Note**
> Many doctors think that women and men forty years of age and older should have a full medical checkup (examination) once a year.

B. Match.

1. A pediatrician
2. An allergist
3. An obstetrician/gynecologist
4. An optometrist
5. A psychologist
6. A dermotologist

- checks my eyes.
- takes care of my children.
- helps me talk about personal problems.
- checks my skin.
- takes care of women.
- helps me control my allergies.

C. Pair practice.

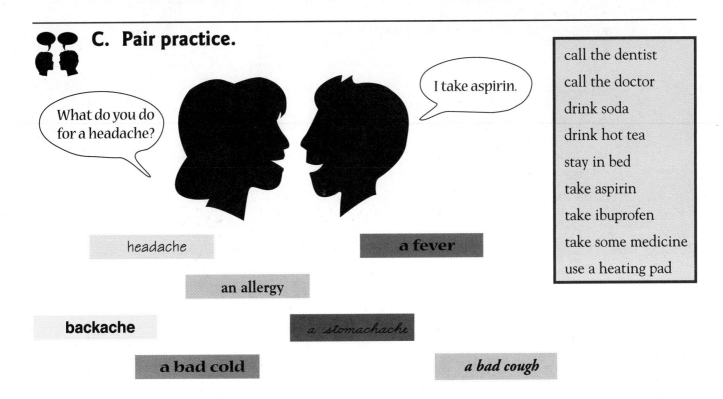

What do you do for a headache?

I take aspirin.

headache

a fever

an allergy

backache

a stomachache

a bad cold

a bad cough

call the dentist
call the doctor
drink soda
drink hot tea
stay in bed
take aspirin
take ibuprofen
take some medicine
use a heating pad

Making an Appointment

A. Read.

Receptionist:	Hello, Dr. Walsh's office.
Patient:	Hello. My daughter is sick.
Receptionist:	What's the problem?
Patient:	She has a high fever and a sore throat.
Receptionist:	Can you come in today at 2:00?
Patient:	Yes, I can.
Receptionist:	What's your name?
Patient:	Mrs. Gonzales.
Receptionist:	Okay, Mrs. Gonzales. The doctor can see you at 2:00.

Culture Note
In a medical emergency, call 911. For a serious illness, call your doctor or clinic. Tell the nurse or receptionist that the problem is serious.

B. Pair practice.

Receptionist: Hello. Dr. _____'s office.

Patient: _____

Receptionist: What's the problem?

Patient: _____

Receptionist: Can you come in today at _____?

Patient: _____

Receptionist: What's _____?

Patient: _____

Receptionist: Okay, _____. The doctor can see you at _____.

Looking at Forms
Patient Information Form

A. Complete.

Culture Note
When you visit a doctor's office for the first time, you will have to fill out an information form or a medical history form.

Patient Information Form

Last Name _____ First Name _____ MI _____

Address _____

City _____ State _____

Zip Code _____

Home Telephone: _____ – _____ – _____

Work Telephone: _____ – _____ – _____

Employer _____

Insurance Company _____

Policy Number _____

Do you have any allergies to medication?   Yes   No

Explain _____

What is your problem today?

_____

_____

The Big Picture: In the Waiting Room

A. Listen.

B. Listen again and number.

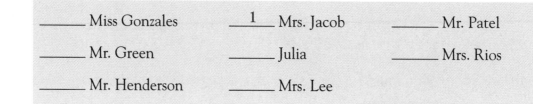

_____ Miss Gonzales	_1_ Mrs. Jacob	_____ Mr. Patel
_____ Mr. Green	_____ Julia	_____ Mrs. Rios
_____ Mr. Henderson	_____ Mrs. Lee	

C. Read and circle.

1. Mrs. Jacob is talking to a patient.   (Yes)   No

2. Mrs. Lee has a headache.   Yes   No

3. Mr. Green has a cold.   Yes   No

4. Mrs. Rios has an allergy.   Yes   No

5. Julia's finger hurts.   Yes   No

6. Mr. Patel has a bad back.   Yes   No

7. Miss Gonzales' throat hurts.   Yes   No

8. Mr. Henderson is holding his stomach.   Yes   No

D. Complete.

1. Mrs. Lee has a _____*cough*_____.

2. Mr. Green has a _____.

3. Julia has a _____.

4. Mr. Patel has a _____.

5. Miss Gonzales has an _____.

6. Mr. Henderson has a _____.

> allergy
>
> backache
>
> burn
>
> cold
>
> ✓ cough
>
> headache

E. Listen and circle.

1. (a.) Yes, it is.   b. No, it isn't.   c. She's the nurse.

2. a. Mr. Green is.   b. Mrs. Jacob is.   c. Julia is.

3. a. Mrs. Lee does.   b. Miss Gonzales does.   c. Mrs. Rios does.

4. a. Dr. Johnson does.   b. Mr. Green does.   c. Mr. Patel does.

5. a. because her finger hurts   b. because she has a cold   c. because she is coughing

F. Try it out.

Write a conversation between a patient and the nurse.

Write about one patient in the waiting room.

Practicing On Your Own

A. Complete.

1. Mr. Carter _____

2. Caroline _____

3. Ms. Brown _____

4. Mr. Rios _____

5. Mr. Lee _____

B. Put the conversation in order. Then write it.

_____ Hello, this is Mrs. Johnson.

_____ Yes. Can you come in at 4:30?

_____ Terrible. I have a bad cold. Can I see Dr. Brown today?

___1___ Good morning, Dr. Brown's office.

_____ Hi, Mrs. Johnson. How are you?

_____ 4:30? That's fine.

Receptionist: *Good morning, Dr. Brown's office.* _____

Patient: _____

Receptionist: _____

Patient: _____

Receptionist: _____

Patient: _____

Looking at Numbers: Reading a Thermometer

A. Read the temperature.

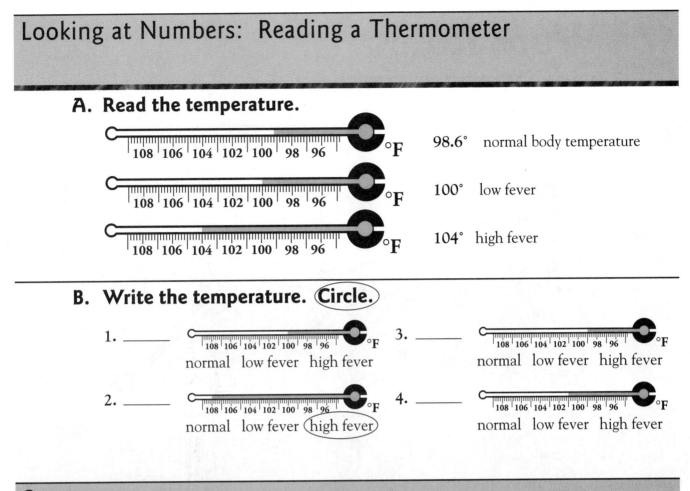

98.6°   normal body temperature

100°   low fever

104°   high fever

B. Write the temperature. (Circle.)

1. _____   normal   low fever   high fever

2. _____   normal   low fever   (high fever)

3. _____   normal   low fever   high fever

4. _____   normal   low fever   high fever

Summary

1. *Have/Has*

I **have** a fever.

You **have** a headache.

We **have** sore throats.

He **has** a stomachache.

She **has** an allergy.

They **have** colds.

2. *My _____ hurts.*

My back **hurts.**

Your knee **hurts.**

Our feet **hurt.**

His arm **hurts.**

Her neck **hurts.**

Their stomachs **hurt.**

3. *When I ..., I...*

When I have a headache, **I** take aspirin.

When they have colds, **they** drink lots of liquids.

4. *Must/Must Not*

An adult **must take** two teaspoons of this medicine.

A child **must not take** this medicine.

Dictionary

A. Listen and repeat.

Jobs

assembler

cable installer

custodian

construction worker

electrician

high-lo driver

landscaper / gardener

machine operator

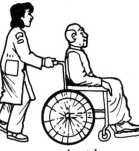
nurse's aide

Tools and equipment

apron

boots

earplugs

earphones

flashlight

forklift

gloves

hair net

hammer

hard hat

mask

mixer

mop

mower

name tag
I.D. badge

safety glasses

screwdriver

shovel

leafblower

sun hat

tool belt

work boots

Grammar in Action

A. Match the equipment with the job.

1. gardener
2. cable installer
3. cook
4. machine operator
5. security guard
6. construction worker
7. custodian
8. high-lo operator
9. nurse's aide

- forklift
- hard hat
- latex gloves
- flashlight
- shovel
- safety glasses
- mop
- mixer
- I.D. badge

B. Pair practice. *Who works at each place below?*

assembler
cable installer
cook
custodian
electrician
gardener
landscaper
machine operator
nurses' aide
high-lo driver

Who works at a factory?

An assembler does.

warehouse

factory

park

apartment building

hospital

school

a private home

hotel

202

C. Listen and (circle.)

1. Jean-Pierre

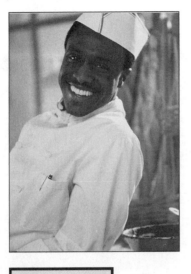

apron
plastic gloves
hat
uniform
mixer
work boots

2. Sue

leafblower
gloves
earphones
flashlight
sun hat
forklift

D. Complete with a partner.

1. An electrician uses a _____ *screwdriver* _____.

2. A construction worker wears a _____.

3. A landscaper uses a _____.

4. A(n) _____ uses earplugs.

5. A(n) _____ wears an I.D. badge.

6. A(n) _____ uses a hammer.

7. At my job, I use _____ and

_____.

8. At my job, I wear _____ and

_____.

Getting to Work Late/Missing Work

A. Listen and write the number.

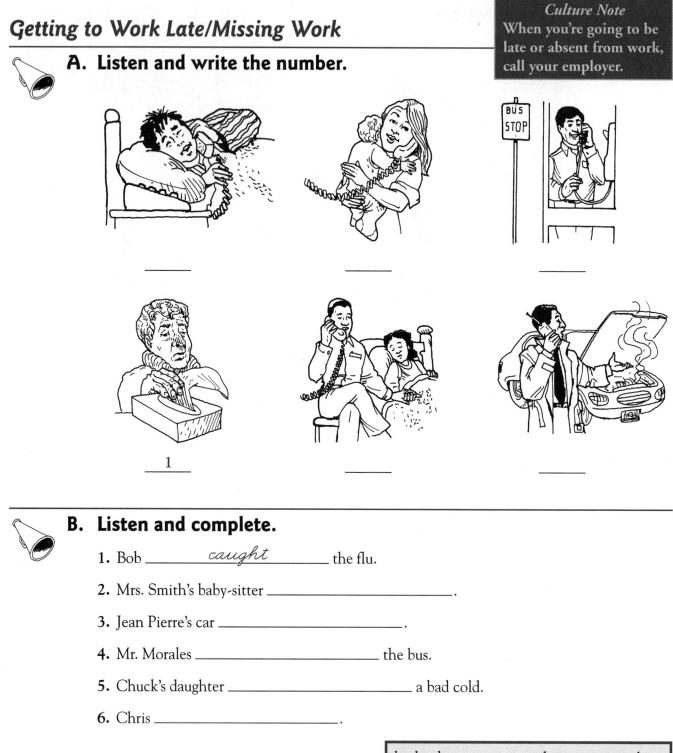

_____   _____   _____

1   _____   _____

B. Listen and complete.

1. Bob _____*caught*_____ the flu.

2. Mrs. Smith's baby-sitter _____.

3. Jean Pierre's car _____.

4. Mr. Morales _____ the bus.

5. Chuck's daughter _____ a bad cold.

6. Chris _____.

broke down	caught	overslept
cancelled	missed	stuck

Working Together: Our Jobs

A. Write the names of four classmates. What are their jobs?

1. Name _____

   He's a(n) _____ .

   He works at _____ .

2. Name _____

   He's a(n) _____ .

   He works at _____ .

3. Name _____

   She's a(n) _____ .

   She works at _____ .

4. Name _____

   She's a(n) _____ .

   She works at _____ .

B. Who is the best worker? Read and discuss.

The worker...	Paul Yes	Paul No	Jean Yes	Jean No	Laura Yes	Laura No
arrives on time.		✔	✔		✔	
learns quickly.		✔	✔		✔	
gets along with other workers.	✔		✔			✔
asks questions.	✔			✔		✔
follows safety rules.	✔		✔		✔	
works carefully.	✔		✔		✔	
works quickly.		✔		✔	✔	

Culture Note
Some companies write job performance reports on their employees every year. A good report may give you a raise (more money) or a promotion (a higher-level job).

C. Interview two students. What do you have to do at work?

Questions	Student 1: _____		Student 2: _____	
1. Do you have to wear a name tag or badge?	Yes	No	Yes	No
2. Do you have to wear a uniform?	Yes	No	Yes	No
3. Do you have to wear safety glasses?	Yes	No	Yes	No
4. Do you have to wear earplugs?	Yes	No	Yes	No
5. Do you have to wear a hair net?	Yes	No	Yes	No
6. Do you have to wear a hard hat?	Yes	No	Yes	No
7. Do you have to wear gloves?	Yes	No	Yes	No
8. Do you have to sign in when you arrive?	Yes	No	Yes	No
9. Do you have to use special equipment?	Yes	No	Yes	No
10. Do you have to use a computer?	Yes	No	Yes	No
11. Do you have to speak English?	Yes	No	Yes	No

D. Complete.

1. _____ has to _____ .
   (Student 1)

2. _____ has to _____ .
   (Student 2)

3. _____ doesn't have to _____ .
   (Student 1)

4. _____ doesn't have to _____ .
   (Student 2)

A. Read.

I'm Cao. I'm a landscaping supervisor. I work six days a week and sometimes seven. I supervise four workers. We have to take care of the lawns and gardens for many homes. As a supervisor, I have to make sure the workers do a good job. Sometimes I have to show a worker how to use equipment. In the winter, we have to clear the snow with shovels and a snowblower. In the spring, we have to plant new flowers and grass. In the summer, we're very busy. We have to cut the lawns, trim the trees, and water the lawns.

I am saving my money because I want to start my own landscaping business.

B. Write about your job or the job of a relative. What do you do at work? What do you have to wear? What are the safety rules?

I work at _____ in _____.
　　　　　　(name of company)　　　　　　　　　(city)

I'm a _____ . I work _____ days a week.
　　　　　　(job)　　　　　　　　　　　　　(number)

I **like / don't like** my job. I wear _____ when I go to work.

When I arrive at work, I always have to _____

_____ . I have to _____

_____ . I have to _____

_____

The Big Picture: Inspection at the Factory

A. Listen.

B. Listen and write.

| Mr. Brooks | Victor | Mei-Lin | Gloria | Anna | Frank | Louise | Vladimir |

C. Listen and ⟨circle.⟩

1. **a.** Yes, it is.
   b. No, it isn't.
   c. It's hot.

2. **a.** He's an employee.
   b. He's the inspector.
   c. He's an assembler.

3. **a.** Victor was.
   b. Vladimir was.
   c. Luis was.

4. **a.** Marie and Mei-Lin were.
   b. Gloria was.
   c. Anna was.

5. **a.** Yes, she was.   **b.** No, she wasn't.   **c.** No, he wasn't.

6. **a.** Luis.   **b.** Anna.   **c.** Joseph.

7. **a.** Joseph.   **b.** Victor.   **c.** Frank and Joseph.

8. **a.** Gloria was.   **b.** Joseph was.   **c.** Louise was.

D. Complete.

Past Continuous
He was wearing...
He wasn't wearing...
They were wearing...
They weren't wearing...

1. Victor _____*was*_____ smoking.

2. Gloria _____ wearing a hair net.

3. Anna _____ wearing safety glasses.

4. Frank and Joseph _____ wearing their hard hats.

5. Vladimir _____ wearing sandals.

6. Louise _____ standing too long.

7. Marie and Mei-Lin _____ wearing gloves.

8. There _____ many safety violations at the factory.

E. Complete.

Have to

I have to	I don't have to
They have to	They don't have to
She has to	She doesn't have to
He has to	He doesn't have to

1. Victor _____*has to*_____ smoke outside the factory.

2. People with long hair _____ wear hair nets.

3. Anna _____ wear safety glasses.

4. Frank and Joseph _____ wear hard hats.

5. I _____ stand all day.

6. I _____ wear a hard hat at my job.

7. I have to _____ at my job.

8. I don't have to _____ at my job.

209

F. Pair practice.

Do	you	have to wear...?
	they	
Does	he	
	she	

Does he have to wear a hard hat?

No, he doesn't.

stand all day

wear a closed shoe

wear gloves

wear a hair net

wear hard hats

wear safety glasses

wear a uniform

1. 2. 3. 4.

Practicing on Your Own

A. Read and complete.

The safety inspector came back to the factory. He was very happy about the workers.

| was _____ ing | were _____ ing |

1. The fire door ____was____ closed.

2. Gloria and Marie ____were____ ____wearing____ hair nets.

3. Vladimir _____ _____ work boots.

4. Luis and Anna _____ _____ safety glasses.

5. Louise _____ _____ in a chair.

6. Wilson _____ _____ his hands.

7. Joseph _____ _____ a hard hat.

8. All of the employees _____ _____ safety rules.

| follow |
| sit |
| wash |
| wear |

B. Match and write.

1. A nurse's aide _____.

2. A cable installer _____.

3. An assembler _____.

4. A construction worker _____.

5. A landscaper _____.

6. A high-lo driver _____.

7. A cook _____.

wears a hard hat and work boots

works in a factory

wears a toolbelt

works with patients and wears a uniform

wears a hairnet

uses a mower

works at a warehouse

211

A. Complete.

Accident Report	
Company Name	Where did the accident occur?
Address	
City State Zip Code	What was the employee doing when the accident happened?
Last Name First Name	
Home Address	
Telephone Social Security No.	
Date of Birth Age Sex / / / M F	Machine, tool, or object that injured the employee
Occupation (Job Title)	
Department (Where employed?)	Illness or part of body affected by injury
Completed by: (Print)	Job Title
Signature	Date

1. Past continuous

I **was wearing** a hard hat.

He **was wearing** a hard hat.

They **were wearing** gloves.

I **wasn't wearing** closed shoes.

He **wasn't wearing** closed shoes.

They **weren't wearing** safety glasses.

2. Past tense

I **missed** the bus.

Regular Verbs: Verb + -ed

cancel   cancel**led**

miss   miss**ed**

He **caught** a cold.

Irregular Verbs

break   **broke**

catch   **caught**

oversleep   over**slept**

3. *Have to/Has to/Don't have to/Doesn't have to*

I **have to wear** a hard hat.

She **has to wear** a hard hat.

They **have to wear** hard hats.

I **don't have to wear** a hard hat.

She **doesn't have to wear** a hard hat.

They **don't have to wear** hard hats.

Do you **have to wear** a hard hat?

Does she **have to wear** a hard hat?

Do they **have to wear** hard hats?

 **School**

Dictionary: In the Classroom

A. Listen and repeat.

Actions

color

cut out pictures

do puzzles

draw

paint a picture

play an instrument

raise his hand

sing

sit in a circle

take a test

work in groups

work on the computer

School subjects

art   foreign language   geography   handwriting

math   music   physical education   science

social studies   spelling

Grammar in Action
School

A. Listen and complete.

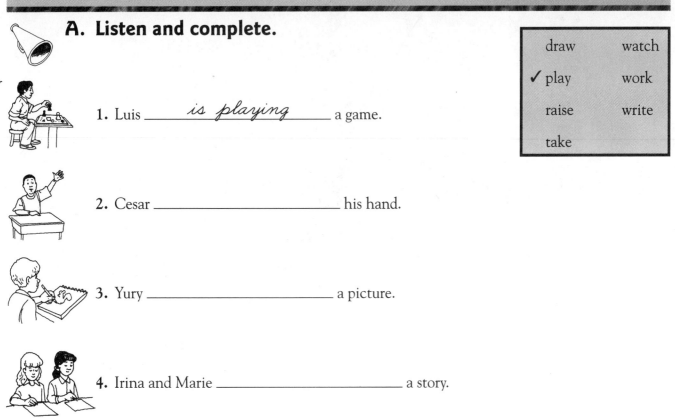

draw	watch
✓ play	work
raise	write
take	

1. Luis _____*is playing*_____ a game.

2. Cesar _____ his hand.

3. Yury _____ a picture.

4. Irina and Marie _____ a story.

215

5. Paul and Michelle _____ a video.

6. Anita _____ a test.

7. Young Su _____ in a group.

B. Match the school subject with the picture.

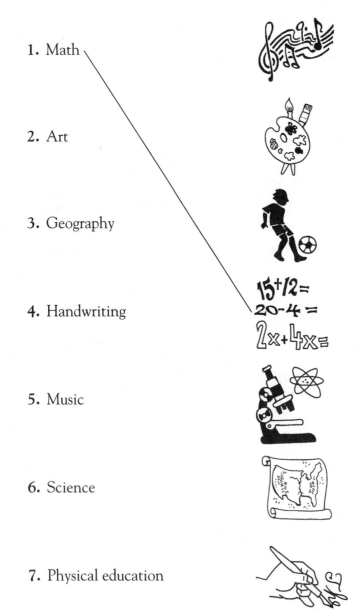

1. Math

2. Art

3. Geography

4. Handwriting

5. Music

6. Science

7. Physical education

C. Pair practice.

color	raise his hand
draw a picture	talk to the teacher
play an instrument	work on the computer

What is Paul doing?

He's drawing a picture.

1.
2.
3.
4.
5.
6.

D. Pair practice.

Did you *work on computers* when you were a child?

Did you *draw* when you were a child?

Past Tense
Did you...?
Yes, I did.
No, I didn't.

Yes, I did.

No, I didn't.

play the piano

color pictures

do puzzles

draw

read books

sing

work on computers

E. **Ask three more questions about your partner's childhood.**

Ordinal Numbers: Grades

A. Listen and repeat.

> *Culture Note*
> Middle school = Grades 6, 7, and 8
> Junior High School = Grades 7, 8, and 9
> Do you have a middle school or a junior high in your town?

kindergarten	**1** first	**2** second	**3** third	**4** fourth	**5** fifth
6 sixth	**7** seventh	**8** eighth	**9** ninth	**10** tenth	**11** eleventh	**12** twelfth

> *Culture Note*
> Children start kindergarten when they are four or five years old.

B. Complete.

Elementary School

1	2	3	4	5
first	_____	_____	_____	_____

Middle School

6	7	8
_____	_____	_____

High School

9	10	11	12
_____	_____	_____	_____

C. Listen and (circle.)

1. elementary   (middle)   high school
2. elementary   middle   high school
3. elementary   middle   high school
4. elementary   middle   high school
5. elementary   middle   high school
6. elementary   middle   high school

D. Complete.

brother	son	grandson	friend
sister	✓ daughter	granddaughter	

1. My _____*daughter*_____ is in the _____*third*_____ grade in _____*elementary*_____ school.

2. My _____ is in the _____ grade in _____ school.

3. My _____ is in the _____ grade in _____ school.

4. My _____ is in the _____ grade in _____ school.

E. Write about your child or a child you know well.

My _____'s School

1. My _____'s school is _____.
                                                        (name of school)

2. My _____ is in the _____ grade.

3. The school is on _____.
                   (street)

4. My _____'s teacher is Mr./Mrs./Ms./Dr. _____.

5. The principal of the school is Mr./Mrs./Ms./Dr. _____.

Culture Note
If you have children, it is important to learn the names of all of your children's teachers. If your child has a problem, call the teacher or the principal.

219

Report Card

A. Listen and complete.

☑ **Her behavior needs improvement.**

doesn't do	doesn't pay	doesn't get along
doesn't follow	✓ doesn't raise	

1. Paula _____*doesn't raise*_____ her hand to answer questions.

2. She _____ attention.

3. She _____ with her classmates.

4. She _____ her homework.

5. She _____ directions.

B. Complete with a partner.

☑ **Excellent behavior**

Present Tense
He raise**s** his hand.
He work**s** in a group.

1. Victor _____*raises*_____ his hand to answer questions.

2. He always _____ his homework.

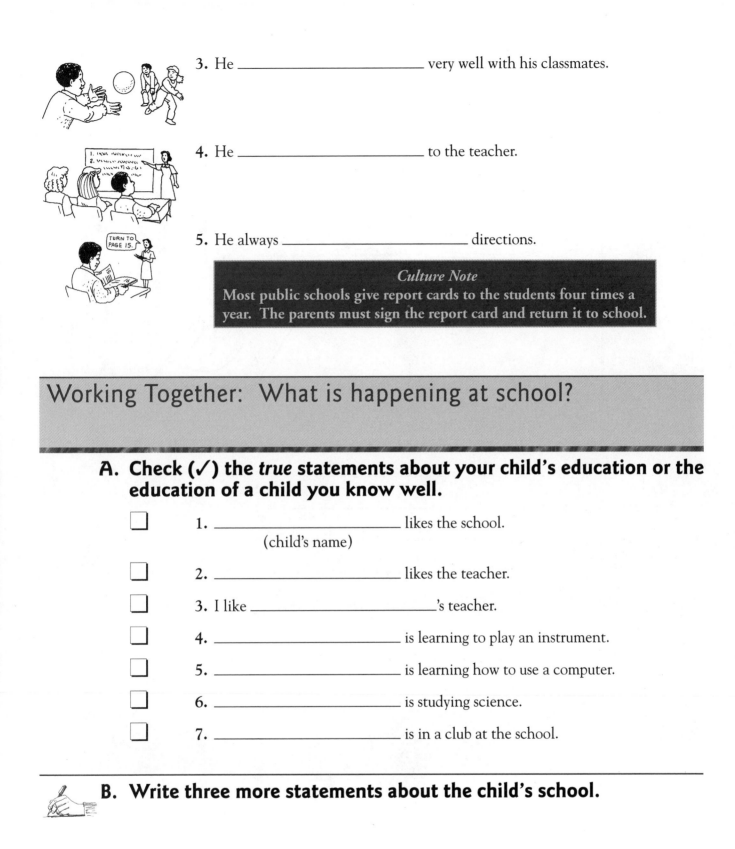

3. He _____ very well with his classmates.

4. He _____ to the teacher.

5. He always _____ directions.

Working Together: What is happening at school?

A. Check (✓) the *true* statements about your child's education or the education of a child you know well.

☐ 1. _____ likes the school.
        (child's name)

☐ 2. _____ likes the teacher.

☐ 3. I like _____'s teacher.

☐ 4. _____ is learning to play an instrument.

☐ 5. _____ is learning how to use a computer.

☐ 6. _____ is studying science.

☐ 7. _____ is in a club at the school.

B. Write three more statements about the child's school.

C. Label the computer with a partner.

CD-ROM

floppy disk

keys

keyboard

monitor

mouse

mouse pad

power switch

screen

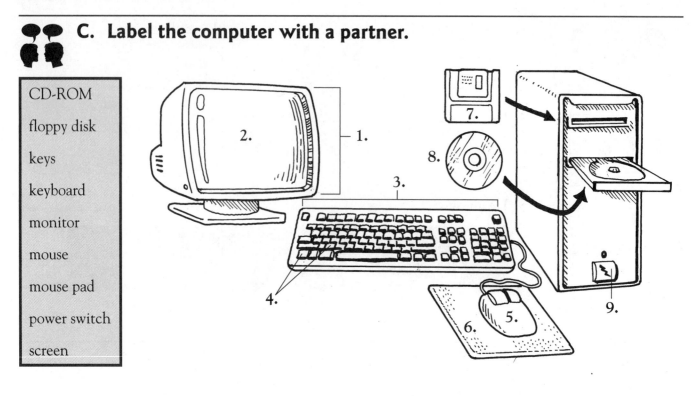

1. _____

2. _____

3. _____

4. _____

5. _____

6. _____

7. _____

8. _____

9. _____

Culture Note
In the U.S., many public schools have computers. Elementary school children practice reading, math, spelling, social studies, and other subjects on computers in their classrooms.

A. Read.

Times Table
6 x 1 = 6
6 x 2 = 12
6 x 3 = 18
6 x 4 = 24

> My son, Nestor Jr., attends Oceanside Elementary School. He's eight years old and in the third grade. He's a good student in English, music, and social studies, but he's not a good math student. I talked to Nestor's teacher, and he said that Nestor needs extra work in math. At the end of the year, there is going to be an important test. Nestor must pass the test. The teacher is going to give him extra homework. I will help him with his times tables.
>
> I want Nestor to do well in school. Maybe he needs a computer at home. Maybe I can learn how to use a computer, too. We can work on the computer together.

B. Write about your child's education, or write about a child you know well.

My _____ is in _____ grade and goes to

_____ school. _____ is good at
(elementary/middle/high)   (name of child)

_____, _____, and _____.

_____

_____

_____

_____

The Big Picture: In the Classroom

A. Listen.

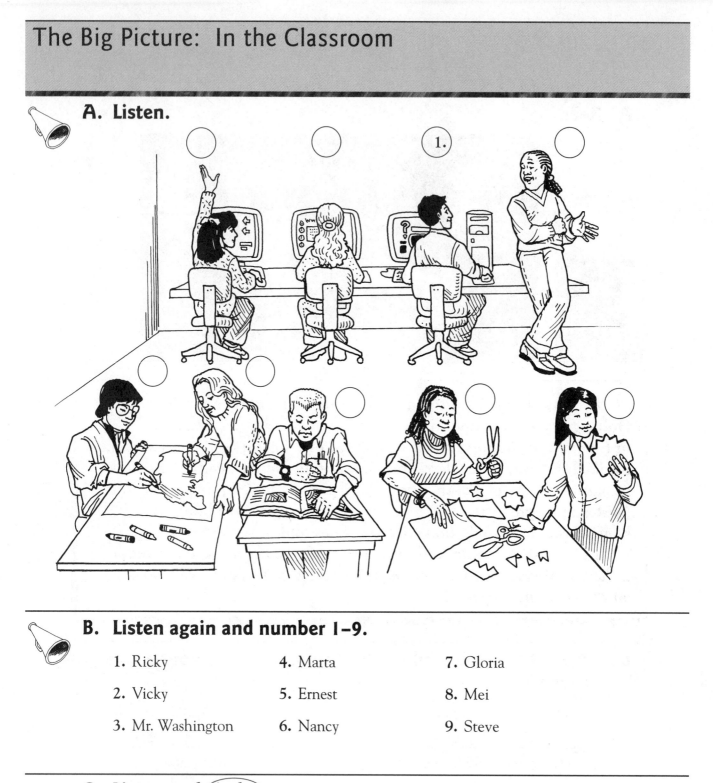

B. Listen again and number 1–9.

1. Ricky
2. Vicky
3. Mr. Washington
4. Marta
5. Ernest
6. Nancy
7. Gloria
8. Mei
9. Steve

C. Listen and circle.

1. Yes No
2. Yes No
3. Yes No
4. Yes No
5. Yes No
6. Yes No
7. Yes No
8. Yes No

D. Complete.

✓ do	help	raise	work
draw	read	sit	

1. The students _____*are doing*_____ final projects.

2. Mr. Washington _____ the students.

3. Almost all of the students _____ in groups.

4. Students _____ on computers.

5. Ernest and Nancy _____ a map.

6. Marta has a question, so she _____ her hand.

7. Steve _____ a magazine; he _____ a book.

8. Gloria and Mei _____ on the computer, but Ricky and Vicky are.

9. Steve _____ alone.

E. Pair practice. *Ask and answer questions about your English class.*

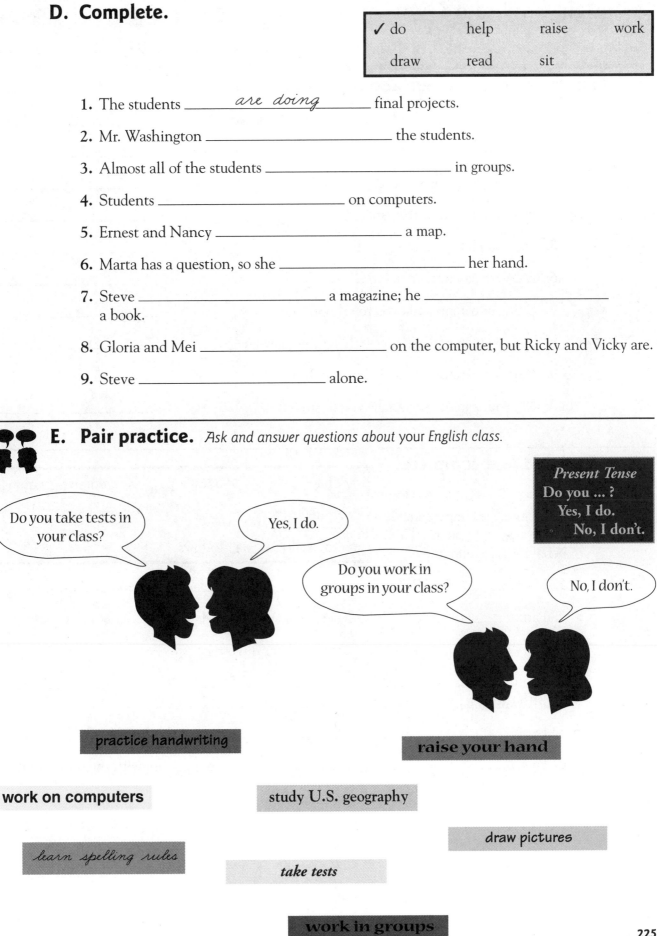

Do you take tests in your class?

Yes, I do.

Do you work in groups in your class?

No, I don't.

Present Tense
Do you ... ?
Yes, I do.
No, I don't.

practice handwriting

raise your hand

work on computers

study U.S. geography

learn spelling rules

take tests

draw pictures

work in groups

Practicing on Your Own

A. Write the answers about your childhood.

1. When you were a child, did you do your homework? _____

2. When you were a child, did you pay attention in class? _____

3. Did you get along with your classmates? _____

4. Did you play an instrument? _____

5. Did you play a sport? _____

6. Did your parents read to you? _____

7. Did your parents walk you to school? _____

8. Did your parents help you with your homework? _____

9. Did your parents talk with your teacher? _____

10. Did your parents encourage you to study? _____

B. Read and complete.

Jason is a poor student. His behavior needs improvement. Patty is a good student. Her behavior is excellent.

doesn't do	✓ doesn't pay	doesn't get along
does	pays	gets along
doesn't follow	follows	

1. Jason _____*doesn't*_____ _____*pay*_____ attention in class.

2. Patty _____ her homework every day.

3. Patty _____ the teacher's directions.

4. Jason _____ _____ _____ with the other students.

5. Jason _____ _____ his homework.

6. Patty _____ _____ well with the other students.

226

Helping Your Child Succeed in School

A. Read.

Read to her.

Help her with her homework.

Give her a quiet place to study.

B. Read this list of ways to help your child in school.

1. Take her to the library.

2. Talk with her teacher regularly.

3. Go on field trips with her.

4. Encourage her to play a musical instrument.

5. Encourage her to play a sport.

C. Write two more ways to help your child in school.

1. _____

2. _____

Looking at Forms: An Absence Note

A. Complete.

_____
(Today's Date)

Dear _____,
       (name of teacher)

_____ could not come to school on _____
       (name of child)   (day of absence)

because she / he _____.
                                           (problem or illness)

Please give her / him the homework.

                                        Sincerely,

                                        _____
                                        (your signature)

Summary

1. Past tense—*Yes/No* questions

Did you **draw** when you were a child?   Yes, I **did.**

Did your parents **read** to you?   No, they **didn't.**

2. Present tense

He **pays** attention.   She **doesn't pay** attention.

He **raises** his hand.   She **doesn't raise** her hand.

3. Present tense—*Yes/No* questions

Do you **have** computers?   Yes, I **do.**

Do you **take** tests?   No, I **don't.**

4. Present continuous

He **is drawing** a picture.

She **is working** on a computer.

They **are sitting** in a circle.

Tape Script

Unit 1: Hello   Page 3

A. Listen.

A: Hello. My name is Jin.
B: Hi. I'm Ana.

A: Nice to meet you.
B: Nice to meet you, too.

Page 4

A. Listen.

ABCDEFGHIJKLMNOPQRSTUVWXYZ

B. Listen again and repeat.

Page 5

A. Listen.

A: What's your first name?
B: Ana.

A: What's your last name?
B: Santos.

A: Please spell that.
B: S - A - N - T - O - S.

Page 7

B. Listen.

a. What's her name?
b. Her name is Ana.
a. Where is she from?
b. She is from Mexico.

a. What's his name?
b. His name is Luis.
a. Where is he from?
b. He is from Colombia.

Page 8

A. Listen.

0 1 2 3 4 5 6 7 8 9 10

B. Listen and repeat.

D. Listen and circle.

a. 1   b. 8   c. 10   d. 0   e. 7   f. 5   g. 9   h. 4   i. 3   j. 6

Page 9

A. Listen.

A: What's your name?
B: Ana Santos.
A: And your telephone number?
B: 301-824-1796.

A: 301-824-1796?
B: Yes.
A: Thank you.

B. Listen and write.

a. 883-3231
b. 654-3692
c. 232-7548

d. 274-3080
e. 201-709-4413
f. 800-442-4242

g. 619-553-7042
h. 813-675-1624

Page 10

A. Listen.

1. Raise your hand.
2. Stand up.
3. Walk to the board.

4. Write your first name.
5. Write your last name.
6. Point to your name.

7. Say your name.
8. Erase your name.
9. Sit down.

B. Listen and find the picture

C. Listen and repeat.

Page 12

A. Listen.

Hi. My name is Tomás. I'm a student in English 1. I'm in class now. Here are four students in my class. This is Hiro. He's from Japan. This is Erica. She's from Mexico. This is Marie. She's from Haiti. This is Jenny. She's from Hong Kong. And this is me. I'm from Peru.

B. Listen again and match the name and the country.

D. Listen. Write the number next to the answer.

1. What's your name?
2. Where are you from?
3. What's his name?
4. Where is he from?
5. What's her name?
6. Where is she from?

Page 16

A. Listen.

A: Good-bye, Ana.
B: Good-bye, Jin.

A: See you tomorrow.
B: Have a nice day.

Unit 2: The Classroom   Page 20

A. Listen. Number the conversations.

1. Is this your book?
   Yes, it is. Thank you.
2. Is this your eraser?
   Yes, it is. Thank you.
3. Is this your pencil?
   No, it isn't.

B. Listen and complete.

1. Is this your dictionary?
   Yes, it is. Thank you.
2. Is this your pen?
   Yes, it is. Thank you.
3. Is this your pencil sharpener?
   No, it isn't.
4. Is this your paper?
   Yes, it is. Thank you.
5. Is this your notebook?
   No, it isn't.

Page 21

A. Listen and repeat.

1. a book   books
2. a pencil   pencils
3. a student   students
4. a man   men
5. a woman   women
6. a child   children

Page 22

A. Listen and circle.

1. a pencil
2. students
3. teachers
4. men
5. a map
6. a dictionary
7. an eraser
8. notebooks
9. classrooms
10. a woman

Page 23

A. Listen.

B. Listen and repeat.

C. Listen and point to the number.

21, 5, 8, 13, 27, 15, 10, 22, 11, 3, 27, 25, 12, 8, 30, 9, 20

D. Listen and circle.

a. 5 b. 9 c. 4 d. 3 e. 17 f. 16 g. 17 h. 11 i. 27 j. 29 k. 26 l. 21

A. Listen.

1. There is a dictionary on the desk.
2. There's a piece of paper on the desk.
3. There are two pencils on the desk.
4. There are five books on the desk.
5. There's an eraser on the desk.
6. There's a notebook on the desk.
7. There's a pen on the desk.

B. Look at the desk. Listen and circle.

1. There are four pencils on the desk.
2. There is a dictionary on the desk.
3. There are two pieces of paper on the desk.
4. There is a pencil sharpener on the desk.
5. There are six books on the desk.
6. There is a pen on the desk.

The Big Picture: The Classroom

B. Listen.

I am a student in English 1. My classroom is on the second floor in Room 204. There are ten students in my class. There are four men and six women. We are from many different countries. There are five students from Mexico. There are two students from Vietnam. There is one student from El Salvador, one from Korea, and one from the Philippines.

Our room is small. There is a big table in the front for the teacher. There are twelve desks for the students. There is a chalkboard on the wall. There are two maps on the wall, one of the United States and one of the world.

Our teacher is Mr. Wilson. We like our teacher, and we like our class.

C. Listen and circle.

1. The classroom is in Room 208.
2. There are twelve students in this class.
3. There are ten men in this class.
4. There are six women in this class.
5. There are four children in this class.
6. There are five students from India.
7. There is one student from El Salvador.
8. The room is small.
9. There are two maps on the wall.
10. We like our class.

Unit 3: Family   Page 33

A. Listen.

Hi. That's me in the first picture. My name is Carlos. This is my family. This is my wife. Her name is Maria. These are my children. I have two sons and one daughter. Robert is 14, George is 11, and Katie is 6. These are my parents. Roberto and Silvia. And these are my two brothers, Tomás and Eric. Tomás is 20 and Eric is 24.

B. Listen again and complete.

A. Listen and read.

Margaret: This is my son Paul.
Kathy: How old is he?
Margaret: He's 7. And this is my daughter, Gloria.
Kathy: How old is she?
Margaret: She's 16.
Kathy: You have a beautiful family.

C. Listen to the conversations. Number the photos.

Picture 1:   A: This is my daughter, Lena. She's 22. And this is her husband,
Charles. He's 25. They live in Florida.
B: Do they have any children?
A: No, they don't.

Picture 2:   This is my husband, Tony. Tony is thirty-two years old. He's a computer salesman.
Picture 3:   This is my son, Mario. He's 22. He's a college student.
Picture 4:   A: This is my daughter, Laura, and her little girl. Her name is
                    Katie and she's six years old. She's our first grandchild.
               B: How old is Laura?
               A: She's 28.

Page 36

A. Listen and read.

Phoung: I have two brothers and one sister. One brother lives in Vietnam and one brother lives in New York.
Linda: Where does your sister live?
Phoung: She lives in Texas.

Page 38

A. Listen.

A: What's your date of birth?   A: What's your birth date?
B: September 14, 1975.   B: March 3, 1980.

B. Listen and repeat.

first – second – third – fourth – fifth – sixth – seventh – eighth – ninth – tenth – eleventh – twelfth –
thirteenth – fourteenth – fifteenth – sixteenth – seventeenth – eighteenth – nineteenth – twentieth –
twenty first – twenty second – twenty third – twenty fourth – twenty fifth – twenty sixth – twenty seventh –
twenty eighth – twenty ninth – thirtieth – thirty first

C. Listen. Write the date.

1. January 4, 1997   5. August 18, 1957
2. February 11, 1982   6. September 7, 1964
3. April 17, 1976   7. November 30, 1999
4. July 25, 1990   8. December 25, 2000

Page 40

A. Listen to Margaret talk about her family. Write the ages of her children.

Hello. My name is Margaret and this is my family. I'm married and my husband's name is Frank. Frank and I live in
Dallas, Texas. We have three children, two boys and one girl. Paul is the oldest; he's 26 years old. He's married and he
and his wife, Diana, live in California. We are grandparents. Paul and Diana have a little boy, Bobby. He's two years old.
Our son Steve is 23 years old and he's single. Steve lives in Florida. Our daughter is in high school. Her name is Gloria
and she's 16 years old.

C. Listen and circle.

1. Margaret and Frank are married.   6. Margaret is a grandmother.
2. They have three sons.   7. Steve is 23 years old.
3. Paul is single.   8. He lives in Florida.
4. He has a son.   9. Gloria is their daughter.
5. Paul lives in Texas.   10. She's married.

Unit 4: At Home   Page 46

A. Listen and complete.

This is our new house. We're moving in today. There is a nice kitchen and a small dining room. There is a
large living room. Upstairs, there are three bedrooms. My daughter is very happy. Now she has her own bedroom.

Page 47

A. Listen.

A: Where do you want this armchair?   A: Where do you want this lamp?
B: Put the armchair in the living room.   B: Put the lamp in Jenny's bedroom.

A. Listen and repeat.
1. He is eating.
2. She is washing the car.
3. He is cooking dinner.
4. They are playing video games.
5. She is using the computer.
6. They are studying.
7. She is sleeping.
8. They are watching TV.
9. He is reading.

C. Listen. Write the number of the correct picture.
1. They are are studying.
2. She is washing the car.
3. He is eating.
4. She is sleeping.
5. They are watching TV.
6. He is reading.
7. He is cooking dinner.
8. They are playing video games.
9. She is using the computer.

Page 50

A. Listen and read.
A: What's your address?
B: 419 South Avenue.

A: What town?
B: Cranford.

A: And what's your zip code?
B: 07016.

B. Listen. Repeat the street addresses.
1. 56 Main Street
2. 37 Maple Street
3. 244 Second Street
4. 872 Central Avenue
5. 1524 Park Avenue
6. 2759 North Avenue

C. Listen. Write the address.
1. 73 North Avenue
2. 66 Maple Street
3. 143 Central Avenue
4. 861 Park Avenue
5. 9924 First Street
6. 3285 Main Street

Page 54

The Big Picture: Where is everybody?

A. Listen to the conversation between Tommy and his mother.
Tommy: Hello.
Mom: Hi, Tommy. This is Mommy.
Tommy: Hi, Mommy. Are you at work?
Mom: Yes, I'm a little late. What are you doing? Are you doing your homework?
Tommy: No, I'm not. I'm watching TV.
Mom: Where's Brian? Is he doing his homework?
Tommy: Brian's in the living room. He's playing video games.
Mom: And Katie? Where's Katie?
Tommy: She's in her bedroom.
Mom: Good! Is she doing her homework?
Tommy: No, Mom. She's talking on the telephone to her boyfriend.
Mom: Where's Daddy? Is he cooking dinner?
Tommy: Daddy's in the living room. He's sleeping.
Mom: I'm coming home right now.

B. Listen again and write the names on the picture.

Page 55

D. Listen and circle.
1. Where is Mom?
2. Where is Tommy?
3. What's he doing?
4. Where is Katie?
5. What's she doing?
6. Where is Dad?
7. What's he doing?

E. Listen and write.
1. Is Mom at home?
2. Is she talking to Tommy?
3. Is Tommy doing his homework?
4. Is Brian doing his homework?
5. Is Brian playing video games?
6. Is Katie doing her homework?
7. Is Dad cooking dinner?
8. Is Dad sleeping?

A. Listen and complete.

1. bakery
2. bank
3. coffee shop
4. supermarket
5. Laundromat
6. drugstore
7. bookstore
8. shoe store

C. Listen and fill in the prepositions.

1. The supermarket is across from the bank.
2. The library is behind the bank and the coffee shop.
3. The bank is on the corner of First and Main Streets.
4. The post office is between the bank and the coffee shop.
5. The bakery is next to the park.
6. The Laundromat is on Second Street.
7. The bakery is across from the parking lot.
8. The bookstore is on the corner of Main Street and Second Street.

Page 66

A. Listen to the story.

It's a busy afternoon downtown. People are busy, and the stores are busy, too. Oh, look! There's an accident at the intersection of Smith Street and North Main Street. Mr. Thomas works at the bakery, and he drives the delivery truck. He's talking to the other driver. Over in the park, Elena is watching the children. The children are playing on swings. The children are having a good time. There's a coffee shop on North Main Street. There are three tables in front of the coffee shop. Joseph is sitting at a table. He's reading the newspaper and drinking a cup of coffee. Jane is sitting at the other table. She's reading a good book. Mark is the waiter. He's bringing Jane some ice cream. Uh, oh. Mrs. Lee is running to her car. Officer Ortiz is standing next to her car. He's writing her a ticket. Oh, how wonderful! Michael and Luisa are in front of City Hall. I think they're getting married today.

B. Listen and circle.

1. Who is watching the children?
2. Who is getting married?
3. Who is standing at the corner of Smith Street and North Main Street?
4. Who is running?
5. Who is working at a coffee shop?
6. Who is reading a book?
7. Who is sitting at the coffee shop?
8. Who is writing a ticket?

Page 67

E. Listen and write.

1. Mr. Thomas **is talking** to the other driver.
2. Elena **is watching** the children.
3. The children **are playing.**
4. They **are having** a good time.
5. Joseph and Jane **are sitting** at tables.
6. Joseph **is reading** a newspaper.
7. Mark **is working** at the coffee shop.
8. Michael and Luisa **are getting** married.

A. Listen and write the job.

1. A: Where does Luis work?
   B: He works at Cosimo's.
   A: What does he do?
   B: He's a waiter.
2. A: Where does Sheri work?
   B: She works at Hair Plus.
   A: What does she do?
   B: She's a manicurist.
3. A: Where does Sandra work?
   B: She works at The Parkside Mall.
   A: What does she do?
   B: She's a custodian.
4. A: Where does Carlos work?
   B: He works at The Clothes Closet.
   A: What does he do?
   B: He's a cashier.

5. A: Where does Ahmed work?
   B: He works at The Parkside Mall.
   A: What does he do?
   B: He's a security guard.
6. A: Where does Marie work?
   B: She works at Family Pharmacy.
   A: What does she do?
   B: She's a pharmacist.
7. A: Where does Richard work?
   B: He works at Hair Plus.
   A: What does he do?
   B: He's a beautician.

Page 78

B. Listen and match.

Conversation 1
A: Where do you work?
B: I work at Cosimo's.
A: What do you do there?
B: I take orders and bring food.
A: Do you like your job?
B: Yes, I do.

Conversation 2
A: Where do you work?
B: I work at The Parkside Mall.
A: What do you do there?
B: I walk around the mall and I watch customers. I'm a security guard there.

Conversation 3
A: Where do you work?
B: I work at Hair Plus.
A: Oh, I know Hair Plus—the beauty parlor in The Parkside Mall.
B: Yes. That's right.

A: What do you do there?
B: I cut nails; I color nails.
A: Do you like your job?
B: Yes. I can sit all day and talk to people.

Conversation 4
A: Where do you work?
B: I work at Family Pharmacy.
A: Oh. I shop there all the time. What do you do there?
B: I fill prescriptions and talk to customers. They ask a lot of questions.

A. Listen and repeat.

two o'clock	two forty
two oh-five	two forty-five
two ten	two fifty
two fifteen	two fifty-five
two thirty	three o'clock

Page 79

C. Listen and show the time on the clocks.
a. four o'clock
b. six thirty
c. eight fifteen
d. ten fifty-five

Page 80

A. Listen and repeat.
Sunday   Monday   Tuesday   Wednesday   Thursday   Friday   Saturday

The Big Picture: The CD Den

B. Listen. Then complete.

My name is Eric. I'm the manager of the CD Den in the Summit Mall. We sell CDs and tapes of all kinds of music—rock, pop, jazz, classical. We have the music you want. In our store, there is always music playing.

The CD Den is open seven days a week from 10:00 AM to 9:00 PM. I work full time, about 50 hours a week. My assistant manager, Mei-Lin, also works full time. All the other employees are part time. We have 10 part-time workers. Most of them are high school and college students. They work about 15 to 20 hours a week, after school and on the weekends. Those are our busiest times. On weekends, we have a security guard, too. She is young, and she doesn't wear a uniform. She looks like a customer. She walks around the store and watches people.

C. Listen. Write the day and times.

1. **Eric:** James, can you work Monday?
   James: What time Monday?
   Eric: From 5:00 to 9:00.
   James: Sure. 5:00 to 9:00. That's okay.
2. **Eric:** Gloria, I need someone Tuesday, from 3:00 to 7:00. Can you work then?
   Gloria: Tuesday. 3:00 to 7:00. No problem. I can work.
3. **Eric:** Makiko, I need another person Saturday. Can you work this Saturday from 10:00 to 5:00?
   Makiko: Yes, I can work Saturday.
4. **Eric:** Andre, can you work Sunday from 10:00 to 6:00?
   Andre: I can't start at 10:00. I can start at 12:00.
   Eric: Okay. Sunday, from 12:00 to 6:00? That's good.
5. **Eric:** Lucy, can you work Friday this week? I need you from 5:00 to 10:00.
   Lucy: That's good for me. I can work Friday.

D. Listen and answer.

1. Does James work Saturday?
2. Does James work Sunday?
3. Does James work full time?
4. Does Lucy work Saturday?
5. Does Lucy work Tuesday?
6. Does Lucy work 15 hours a week?

Unit 7: Money   Page 92

A. Listen and repeat.

a. four cents
b. ten cents
c. twenty-five cents
d. thirty cents
e. thirty-five cents
f. fifty cents
g. sixty-two cents
h. seventy-five cents
i. eighty-five cents
j. ninety-nine cents

D. Listen and write the amount.

a. two cents
b. ten cents
c. seventeen cents
d. twenty-five cents
e. thirty-eight cents
f. forty-nine cents
g. fifty cents
h. sixty-nine cents
i. ninety-eight cents

A. Listen and repeat.

a. one dollar
b. one dollar and fifty cents
c. two seventy-five
d. four ninety-nine
e. seven thirty-seven
f. nine eighty-five
g. twelve ninety-eight
h. twenty-four ninety-five
i. seventy-seven twenty

C. Listen and write the amount.

a. a dollar
b. a dollar twenty-five
c. a dollar ninety-eight
d. two dollars and fifty cents
e. three dollars and seventy-five cents
f. fifteen dollars and eight cents
g. thirty-six eighty-five
h. fifty-seven sixty-two
i. ninety-five twenty-six

B. Listen and write the price on each item above.

Conversation 1
A: How much is the microwave?
B: It's $99.
A: $99? Let's buy it.

Conversation 2
A: How much is this pot?
B: It's $12.99.
A: Hmm. $12.99. That's a good price.

Conversation 3
A: How much is the rice cooker?
B: It's $27.95.
A: $27.95? That's expensive.

Conversation 4
A: How much is the coffeemaker?
B: It's on sale. It's $14.49.
A: We need a coffeemaker. Let's buy it.
B: Yeah. $14.49 is a good price.

Conversation 5
A: How much is this wok?
B: It's $22.98.
A: $22.98. That's a lot. But we need a wok and this is a good one.

Conversation 6
A: How much is the teakettle?
B: It's on sale for $23.
A: That's a sale? $23?
B: That's too expensive.

B. Listen and write the price on each item in Part A.

Conversation 1
A: How much are the spoons?
B: They're $1.00 each.
A: $1.00 each! That's a good price. Let's buy six.

Conversation 2
A: How much are the dishes?
B: They're $39.99
A: Hmm. $39.99. That's a good price.

Conversation 3
A: How much are the glasses?
B: They're $19.99.
A: We need glasses and that's a good price.

Conversation 4
A: How much are the pot holders?
B: They're on sale. They're $6.00 each.
A: We don't need any pot holders.

Conversation 5
A: How much are the mugs?
B: They're $7.99 each.
A: $7.99. That's too expensive.

Conversation 6
A: How much are the knives?
B: They're $10.00 each.
A: We need some good knives. Let's buy six.

The Big Picture: A Yard Sale

B. Listen to the story.

Tuan and Lana are moving from an apartment to a house. They're looking for furniture and other items they need for their new home. They need a microwave for the kitchen. They have another bedroom, so they need a bed and a dresser. Tuan and Lana have a list of yard sales from the local newspaper. They are going to stop at five or six yard sales this morning. This yard sale has a lot of furniture and kitchen items. Tuan is asking the owner about the dresser. Lana is looking at the microwave. Their two little boys are with them. Michael wants some action figures, and Dustin is playing with a toy truck.

D. Listen and circle. How much are they going to pay?

1. **A:** How much is this wok?
   B: It's $5.00.
   A: How about $3.00.
   B: It's a good wok. $4.00.
   A: Okay. $4.00.
2. **A:** How much is that toy truck?
   B: That little truck? It's a dollar.
   A: Good. Here's a dollar.
3. **A:** Does this microwave work?
   B: Yes, it works fine. I bought a new one because that's too small. But it's a good microwave.
   A: $25.00 is high. I'll give you $15.
   B: How about $20.
   A: Okay. Here's $20.
4. **A:** How much are these glasses?
   B: $5.00.
   A: For all of them?
   B: Yes. $5.00 for all the glasses.
5. **A:** How much is this dresser?
   B: It's $25.00.
   A: And the bed?
   B: It's $25.
   A: $50. Hmm. I'll give you $30 for both the bed and the dresser.
   B: Hmm. How about $40?
   A: Okay.
6. **A:** How much are the action figures?
   B: They're a dollar each.
   A: Okay. Michael, you can have two action figures. Here's $2.00.

Unit 8: Shopping and Recreation   Page 108

C. Listen. Write the letter of the picture above next to the number.

You will hear: Example: 1. She's wearing shoes.

2. She's wearing a hat.
3. She's wearing jeans.
4. She's wearing a belt.
5. She's wearing a skirt.
6. She's wearing sandals.

Page 112

A. Listen.

1. Walk into the store.
2. Look at the jackets.
3. Try on a jacket.
4. Look in the mirror.
5. It's too big. Try on another one.
6. Look in the mirror again.
7. Take it off.
8. Walk to the cashier.
9. Pay for your jacket.

B. Listen and find the picture.

C. Listen and repeat.

The Big Picture: At the Park

A. Listen.

It's a beautiful spring day in the park. The weather is warm, and there are many people in the park. It's Sunday. There's a pond in the middle of the park, and there are many trees and flowers. Every Sunday afternoon, Mr. Garcia comes to the park with his granddaughter, Suzie. They like to feed the ducks. Mr. and Mrs. Robinson are walking in the park today. They walk in the park three times a week for exercise. Some children are playing in a soccer game. Their parents are watching the game. Jack is riding his bicycle with his parents, Mary and Bill. They're going to ride all around the park. The park is full of activities today.

B. Listen and circle.

1. The weather is warm.
2. There are many people in the park.
3. Today is Tuesday.
4. There's a pond in the middle of the park.
5. Mr. Garcia brings his grandson to the park.
6. Mr. and Mrs. Robinson like to run in the park.
7. They come to the park three times a week.
8. Children are playing soccer in the park.

C. Listen and cicle.

1. What is Hector doing?
2. Is he playing soccer?
3. What is Hector wearing?
4. Where is Gina?
5. What is she doing?
6. What is she wearing?
7. Who is playing soccer?
8. Who is watching the game?

Unit 9: Food   Page 121

B. Listen and look at Exercise A again. Circle the food that Michael likes. Cross out the food that he doesn't like.

Michael eats breakfast at 7:00 in the morning. He likes cereal for breakfast. Sometimes he has pancakes. Michael doesn't like eggs.

Michael eats lunch at work. He eats at 12:30. He usually takes a sandwich to work. Sometimes he takes a salad. He doesn't like soup for lunch.

Michael eats dinner at home. He likes pasta and he likes chicken. Michael doesn't like fish.

B. Listen. Number the orders.

Order number 1:
Waiter: May I take your order?
Customer: A tuna salad sandwich.
Waiter: What kind of bread?
Customer: White, please.
Waiter: Anything to drink?
Customer: Coffee, please.

Order number 2:
Waitress: May I take your order?
Customer: Vegetable soup and a green salad.
Waitress: Anything to drink?
Customer: Iced tea, please.

Order number 3:
Waitress: May I take your order?
Customer: A grilled cheese sandwich.
Waitress: What kind of bread?
Customer: Rye, please.
Waitress: Anything to drink?
Customer: A cola, please.

Order number 4:
Waiter: May I take your order?
Customer: I'll have a hamburger and french fries, please
Waiter: Anything to drink?
Customer: Coffee, please.

A. Listen.

1. Open the menu.
2. Look at the menu.
3. Order a sandwich.
4. Order a drink.
5. Wait for your order.
6. Eat your lunch.
7. Ask for the bill.
8. Pay the bill.
9. Leave a tip.

B. Listen and find the picture.

C. Listen and repeat.

The Big Picture: At the Restaurant

A. Listen.

It's Friday night at Mario's Italian Restaurant. Troy and Erika always eat at Mario's on Friday night. They are sitting at a table near the window. The waitress is taking their order. Erika is looking at the menu. She's ordering a salad and spaghetti. Troy is ordering a salad and chicken. They are both ordering iced tea to drink. Bob and Ann are at the restaurant, too. They are with their two daughters, Lori and Tess. Bob and Ann are tired after working all day and they don't want to cook dinner. They're eating a pizza. They're all drinking soda.

B. Listen again and number.

C. Listen and circle.

1. It's Monday night.
2. Troy and Erika like Mario's Italian Restaurant.
3. Erika is ordering breakfast.
4. Troy is ordering a pizza.
5. Bob and Ann are tired.
6. Bob and Ann are eating out with their daughters.
7. The waitress is taking their order.
8. They are eating sandwiches.

D. Listen and circle.

1. What day is it?
2. Where are Troy and Erika sitting?
3. Who is taking their order?
4. What is Troy ordering?
5. What is the family eating?
6. Are they drinking soda?

Unit 10: Finding an Apartment   Page 134

A. Listen and circle.

1. Is there a kitchen in the apartment?
2. Are there three bedrooms in the apartment?
3. Are there many windows?
4. Is there only one bathroom?
5. Is there a garage?
6. Is there a closet near the door?
7. Is there a washer/dryer in the apartment?

C. Listen and write.

1. The paint is peeling.
2. The ceiling is leaking.
3. A window is stuck.
4. The heat is off.
5. The neighbors are noisy.
6. The electricity is off.
7. There is a mouse in the apartment.

A. Listen. Match the conversation and the problem. Then, circle the time.

Conversation 1
A: Hello, Mr. Williams. This is Mrs. Lopez in Apt. 3C.
B: Hello, Mrs. Lopez.
A: Could you come right away? It's 100 degrees in here. My air conditioner isn't working.
B: Your air conditioner isn't working?
A: That's right.
B: I'll be there right away.

Conversation 2
A: Hello, Mr. Williams. This is Miss DeVico in Apt. 5F.
B: Hello, Miss DeVico.
A: (mouse noise) Aghh! Please come right away! There's a mouse in my kitchen.
B: A mouse in the kitchen?
A: Yes! Aghh! Hurry up!
B: I'm coming right now.

Conversation 3
A: Hello, Mr. Williams. This is Mr. Martins in Apt 14D.
B: Hello, Mr. Martins.

A: The kitchen faucet has a small leak. Can you come look at it?

B: The faucet is leaking? Mr. Martins, I'm very busy today.

A: When can you come fix it?

B: I'll be there tomorrow.

Conversation 4

A: Hello, Mr. Williams. This is Mrs. Walker in 12B.

B: Hello, Mrs. Walker. How are you today?

A: I'm very upset. I'm trying to cook dinner, and the stove isn't working.

B: The stove isn't working?

A: That's right. When can you come fix it?

B: I'm a little busy right now, but I'll be there later.

Conversation 5

A: Hello Mr. Williams. This is Mr. Young in 24A.

B: Hello, Mr. Young.

A: Mr. Williams, I think there's a leak in my ceiling. There's water on the floor.

B: Is it a big leak?

A: I don't think so. There's only a little water on the floor.

B: Okay. I'll be there later this afternoon.

Conversation 6

A: Hi, Mr. Williams. This is Miss Dorisme in 10D.

B: Hello, Miss Dorisme. How are you?

A: Not well. I can't lock my door. I think the lock is broken.

B: I'll be there right away.

Page 142

The Big Picture: My Neighborhood

A. Listen.

Hi, I'm Ana Lee. This is my apartment and my neighborhood. I live in a one-bedroom apartment on the second floor. There's no elevator, so I walk up and down the stairs. I have a small bedroom, but it's very sunny. I have a small bathroom, a living room, and a kitchen. I would like to have a pet, but in my building, you must not have any pets.

I like my neighborhood. It's quiet, safe, and convenient. I'm near everything. The park is across the street, so I walk in the park every morning. I shop at the green market, and I can pay my phone bill at the telephone company. Best of all, I can walk to work because I teach at the elementary school down the street. Finally, I have great neighbors. Mr. and Mrs. Robinson live next door, and my friend, Kevin lives in the apartment on the other side. They're quiet, and they're very friendly.

B. Listen and circle.

1. The apartment is on the fourth floor.
2. The bedroom is small.
3. Ana has a cat.
4. Ana likes her neighborhood.
5. The telephone company is next to her apartment building.
6. Ana works at the post office.
7. Ana takes the bus to work.
8. Ana likes her neighbors.

Page 143

C. Listen and complete.

1. There is one bedroom in the apartment.
2. There is a small kitchen in the apartment.
3. There are many windows in the apartment.
4. There isn't an elevator in the building.
5. There aren't any pets in the building.
6. There's a bank down the street.
7. There is a parking lot near the building.
8. The neighbors are quiet and friendly.

Unit 11: Applying for a Job   Page 151

A. Listen to each person talk about his or her job experience. Write the number of the speaker under each picture.

1. In my country I was a desk clerk. I can use a computer and register guests.
2. In my country I was a cook. I can cook Mexican food and Italian food.
3. In my country, I was a laundry worker. I can wash and fold towels and sheets. I can do the guests' laundry.
4. In my country, I was a piano player. I can play popular music, jazz, rock, all kinds of music.

A. Listen and read.

Alex: I'm applying for a job as a cook.
Manager: Do you have any experience?
Alex: Yes, I was a cook at The Flamingo in Tampa.
Manager: When?
Alex: From 1996 to 2000. And I was a waiter at Tio Pepe in Cancún from 1992 to 1996.

D. Listen and write the salary and benefits.

Conversation 1
Manager: Your salary is $8 an hour. Overtime pay is $10 an hour.
Karina: What are the benefits?
Manager: You have medical benefits after six months. You have 3 sick days and one
week vacation the first year.

Conversation 2
Mohamed: What is the salary?
Manager: The salary is $6 an hour plus tips.
Mohamed: And the benefits?
Manager: For part time employees, there are no benefits.

Conversation 3
Manager: The starting salary is $9 an hour.
Li-Ping: And the overtime pay?
Manager: The overtime pay is the same, $14 an hour.
Li-Ping: Are there medical benefits?
Manager: Yes, there are medical benefits and a prescription plan. You have two sick days and two weeks vacation.

Conversation 4
Manager: The salary is $14 an hour. After six months, it's $16 an hour.
Juan: And the benefits?
Manager: We have a good benefit package here. There's medical and dental and prescription. You have five
sick days and two weeks vacation the first year. The second year, you have three weeks vacation.

B. Listen and check *Yes* or *No*.

Luis: I'm applying for the job as a valet.
Manager: Do you have any experience?
Luis: As a valet, no. I was a cashier at Frank's Fried Chicken.
Manager: Do you have a clean driver's license? Any tickets?
Luis: It's clean. No tickets. No accidents.
Manager: Can you drive a stick shift?
Luis: Yes, I can.
Manager: We need to check your driver's license. When can you start?
Luis: Tomorrow.
Manager: The job is part time. Wednesday and Thursday, 5:00 to 10:00 and Friday, Saturday, and Sunday, 5:00
to 12:00. It pays $3 an hour plus tips.
Luis: OK.
Manager: Wear black slacks and black shoes. We'll give you a red jacket.
Luis: OK. Thank you.

The Big Picture: The Sunrise Hotel
A. Listen and circle.

My name is Ricardo Lopez. This is the Sunrise Hotel, and I'm the evening manager here. The Sunrise is a big hotel with more than 200 rooms. There's a restaurant, a bar, two swimming pools, and tennis courts. The Sunrise is a popular hotel for tourists. We have a lovely location here on the beach.

The hotel has about 100 employees. We have all the regular employees, desk clerks, housekeeping, bellhops, landscapers, the restaurant employees. Then we have other positions, such as the courtesy van drivers who drive guests from the hotel to the airport. We need people around the clock, three shifts. The first shift is from 7:00 AM to 3:00 PM, the second shift is from 3:00 PM to 11:00 PM and the third shift is the night shift; it's from 11:00 PM to 7:00 AM. People who work at night make a dollar an hour extra because it's hard to find people for those hours. We also have many part-time workers.

We are always looking for employees. The salary is low and our employees work hard. When people find a job that pays more, they leave us. But some people stay for a long time. Some workers like the tips. Other workers like the hours. The atmosphere is friendly here. Are you looking for a job? We have several openings.

Page 163

B. Listen. Who is the manager speaking to?
1. Please clean Rooms 371 and 374.
2. Take these bags to Room 433.
3. Table 4 wants more coffee.
4. How many empty rooms do we have tomorrow night?
5. Please get Ms. Butler's car.
6. Some of these towels are not clean. What kind of detergent are we using?
7. The air conditioner in Room 512 isn't working.

Unit 12: Transportation   Page 171

B. Listen and write the locations on the map.
1. **A:** Where's City Hall?
   B: Walk two blocks to Broad Street. Turn left. City Hall is on your right.
2. **A:** Where's the library?
   B: Walk three blocks to the first traffic light. Turn left. The library is two blocks up on your right.
3. **A:** Where's the hospital?
   B: Walk three blocks to the first traffic light. Turn right. The hospital is on your left.
4. **A:** Where's the aquarium?
   B: Walk four blocks to the second traffic light. That's Clark Street. Turn right. The aquarium is on your left.

Page 172

A. Listen.
A: How do I get to the zoo?   **B:** Take the 21 bus. Get off at State Street.

B. Listen and write the bus number. Circle the street name.
Example: **A:** How do I get to the hospital?
    B: Take the 14 Bus. Get off at Jackson Avenue.
a. **A:** How do I get to the airport?
 B: Okay. Take the 49 Bus. And then get off at Maple Street
b. **A:** How do I get to the art museum?
 B: It's easy. Just take the 22 Bus and get off at Clark Avenue.
c. **A:** How do I get to the aquarium?
 B: Take the 10 Bus. And then you need to get off at Fourth Street.
d. **A:** How do I get to the stadium?
 B: You need to take the 18 Bus. Look for Bay Street. That's your stop.
e. **A:** How do I get to City Hall?
 B: You want the 37 Bus. Get off at Central Avenue.

Page 173

A. Listen to the weather. Find the city and write the temperature on the map.
Look at the map of the United States.
Find Boston. It's cold in Boston today. It's snowing. The temperature is 20 degrees.
Find New York. It's cloudy and cold in New York today. The temperature is 35 degrees.
Find Miami. It's sunny and hot in Miami. The temperature is 80 degrees.

Find Houston. It's sunny and warm in Houston today. The temperature is 70 degrees.
Find San Diego. The weather is beautiful in San Diego all year. It's sunny and 75 degrees.
Find San Francisco. It's raining today in San Francisco. It's cool. The temperature is 55 degrees.
Find Seattle. It's raining in Seattle, too. It's 50 degrees in Seattle. You will need your umbrella and raincoat.
Find Denver. It's snowing in Denver today. It's 30 degrees in Denver.
Find Chicago. It's cloudy and cold in Chicago today. It's very windy. The temperature is 25 degrees.

Page 176

A. Listen.
1. Have the exact change.
2. Walk to the bus stop.
3. Wait for the bus.
4. Get on the bus.
5. Pay the exact fare.
6. Ask for a transfer.
7. Sit down.
8. Push the button.
9. Get off the bus.

B. Listen and find the picture.

Page 177

C. Listen and repeat.

Page 180

The Big Picture: Traffic

A. Listen.

It's a beautiful sunny day and everyone is on the road. There are many cars on Route 66 and the traffic is heavy. Bill and Barbara are on the highway. They are going to get off at Exit 12. They're going to watch a soccer game at the stadium. Liz is on the highway, too. She's going to get off at Exit 14. She's going to visit the art museum. Thomas and Eric are driving on the highway, too. They're going to get off at Exit 15. It's a hot day and they're going to the beach. They're going to fish all day.

B. Listen and circle.
1. What's the weather?
2. Where are Barbara and Bill?
3. Where are they going?
4. Where is Liz getting off?
5. What is she going to do?
6. Where are Eric and Thomas?
7. Where are they going?

Page 181

C. Listen and write the road number and the exit number.
1. **A:** How do I get to the football stadium?
   B: Take Highway 76 and get off at Exit 25.
2. **A:** How do I get to the beach?
   B: Take Route 12 East and get off and Exit 9.
3. **A:** How do I get to Green Trees Park?
   B: You need to take Interstate 287 and then get off at Exit 10.
4. **A:** How do I get to the airport?
   B: Get on the freeway. It's 5 North. Get off at Exit 19.
5. **A:** How do I get to the science museum?
   B: Take Route 84 and get off at exit 37.
6. **A:** How do I get to the shopping mall?
   B: Take Highway 66. You'll go about 10 miles, and then get off at Exit 3.

Unit 13: A Visit to the Doctor   Page 189

A. Listen and repeat.
1. Her head hurts.
2. Her back hurts.
3. Her stomach hurts.
4. His ear hurts.
5. His foot hurts.
6. His tooth hurts.

B. Listen again and write.

C. Listen and repeat.
backache
stomachache
earache
toothache
headache

245

Page 191

A. Listen and repeat.
1. Use an ice pack
2. Call the dentist.
3. Take ibuprofen.
4. Call the doctor.
5. Take aspirin.
6. Stay in bed.
7. Use a heating pad.
8. Drink liquids.

Page 196

The Big Picture: In the Waiting Room
A. Listen.

Dr. Johnson's waiting room is very busy. Mrs. Jacob is Dr. Johnson's nurse. She is talking to a patient. Mrs. Lee has a bad cough. Mr. Green is 75 years old, and he has a bad cold. Mrs. Rios' daughter, Julia, is crying. Her finger hurts. She has a bad burn. Mr. Patel is holding his head because he has a terrible headache. Miss Gonzales has very bad allergies. She's coughing and sneezing. Mr. Henderson feels very uncomfortable because his back hurts. Everyone feels terrible!

B. Listen again and number.

Page 197

E. Listen and circle.
1. Is the waiting room busy?
2. Who is talking to the patients?
3. Who has a bad cough?
4. Who has a headache?
5. Why is Julia crying?

Unit 14: Work Rules   Page 203

C. Listen and circle.
1. Hi, I'm Jean-Pierre. I'm a pastry chef in a French restaurant. When I am at work, I always wear a white uniform. I always wear a hat to cover my hair. Sometimes I wear plastic gloves. I use a mixer when I make cakes.
2. Hi, I'm Sue. I'm a gardener. In the summer, I wear a big sun hat. In the spring and summer, I plant a lot of flowers, so I usually wear gloves. In the fall, I have to use a leafblower to clean the leaves, and I usually wear earphones because the leafblower is really noisy.

Page 204

A. Listen and write the number.
Conversation 1
A: Hello, Mr. Berman's office.
B: Hello, (cough, cough). This is Bob.
A: Hello, Bob. You sound terrible!
B: (Cough, cough) I have the flu. I can't come to work today.
A: Okay. I'll tell your supervisor.
B: Thank you. (Achoo!) Bye.
Conversation 2
A. Hello, may I speak to Mr. Lee?
B: Speaking.
A: Hello, Mr. Lee, this is Beth Smith.
B: Hello, Mrs. Smith.
A: Mr. Lee, I'm going to be late to work today.
B: What's the problem, Mrs. Smith?
A: My baby-sitter cancelled. I have to take my baby to my mother's house.
B: Alright. Be here as soon as you can.
A: I will. Good-bye.

Conversation 3

A: Hello, Super Auto Company.

B: Hello, Mr. Tanaka, please.

A: He's in a meeting. May I take a message?

B: Yes, this is Jean Pierre. My car broke down, so I'm going to be late.

A: When are you going to be here?

B: In about an hour.

A: Alright. I'll tell Mr. Tanaka.

B: Thank you. Good-bye.

Conversation 4

A: Hello, Tea and Coffee Corporation.

B: Hello, may I speak to Mrs. James, please?

A: Speaking.

B: Hello, Mrs. James. This is Rob Morales.

A: Hello, Rob.

B: Uh, I'm going to be late to work this morning.

A: Late again? You were late yesterday!

B: I'm sorry, but I missed the bus.

A: You missed the bus? If you're not here by 10:00, you're fired. Good-bye!

Conversation 5

A: Hello, Hues Corporation.

B: Hello, may I speak to Mr. Reynolds?

A: He's busy right now. May I take a message?

B: Yes, this is Chuck Williams. I'm not going to be at work today.

A: Why not?

B: My daughter caught a bad cold and has a fever. I have to take her to the doctor. I think I should stay home with her today.

A: Okay. I'll tell Mr. Reynolds.

B: Thank you. Good-bye.

Conversation 6

A: Hello?

B: Hello, may I speak to Chris Ward?

A: Speaking. Who is this?

B: Chris, this is Joana. Are you coming to work today?

A: What time is it?

B: It's 8:45.

A: 8:45 . . . 8:45! Oh, no! I overslept! I'm sorry! I'll be there in fifteen minutes!

B. Listen and complete.

1. Bob caught the flu.
2. Mrs. Smith's baby-sitter cancelled.
3. Jean Pierre's car broke down.
4. Mr. Morales missed the bus.
5. Chuck's daughter caught a bad cold.
6. Chris overslept.

Page 208

The Big Picture: Inspection at the Factory

A. Listen.

It's a very hot, summer day. The toy truck factory is very busy. They're making trucks for next Christmas. Today is a bad day for the factory and for the manager. The manager, Mr. Brooks, is listening to the inspector, Mr. DiMauro. There are many problems in the factory. Mr. DiMauro has a long list of work safety violations. Victor was smoking in a no-smoking area. Marie and Mei-Lin were wearing hair nets, but Gloria wasn't. Gloria was wearing gloves, but Marie and Mei-Lin weren't. Ana wasn't wearing safety glasses. In the hard hat area, Frank and Joseph weren't wearing their hard hats. Louise is six months pregnant, and she was still standing up. She looked very tired. Vladimir was wearing sandals. Finally, the fire door was open. Mr. Brooks looks very upset. He will to have to pay a big fine.

B. Listen and write.

C. Listen and circle.

1. Is the factory busy?
2. Why is Mr. DiMauro at the factory today?
3. Who was smoking?
4. Who was wearing a hair net?
5. Was Vladimir wearing work boots?
6. Who wasn't wearing safety glasses?
7. Who wasn't wearing a hard hat?
8. Who was very tired?

A. Listen and complete.
1. Luis is playing a game.
2. Cesar is raising his hand.
3. Yury is drawing a picture.
4. Irina and Marie are writing a story.
5. Paul and Michelle are watching a video.
6. Anita is taking a test.
7. Young Su is working in a group.

Page 218

A. Listen and repeat.

kindergarten	first	second
third	fourth	fifth
sixth	seventh	eighth
ninth	tenth	eleventh
twelfth		

Page 219

C. Listen and circle.
1. seventh grade
2. fourth grade
3. tenth grade
4. kindergarten
5. eleventh grade
6. eighth grade

Page 220

A. Listen and complete.
1. Paula doesn't raise her hand to answer questions.
2. She doesn't pay attention.
3. She doesn't get along with her classmates.
4. She doesn't do her homework.
5. She doesn't follow directions.

Page 224

The Big Picture: In the Classroom
A. Listen.

This is Mr. Washington's seventh-grade social studies class. It is almost the end of the school year, so everyone is busy. Almost all of the students are working in groups. They are doing their final projects for the class. Ricky and Vicky are working on computers. Mr. Washington is helping them. Marta is also working on a computer. She has a question, so she is raising her hand. Ernest and Nancy are drawing a map. Gloria and Mei are using scissors to make a picture. Steve isn't sitting with a group because he doesn't like to work in groups. He is reading a magazine and writing. It is a very noisy classroom, but the students are working hard.

B. Listen again and number 1–9.

C. Listen and circle.
1. This is a sixth-grade class.
2. Mr. Washington is helping the students.
3. Ernest is drawing a map.
4. Ricky is raising his hand.
5. Mei is painting a picture.
6. Steve is reading with a group of students.
7. Steve likes to work in groups.
8. Some of the students are working in groups.